T0352626

Favorite Flies for

PENNSYLVANIA

Favorite Flies for

PENNSYLVANIA

50 ESSENTIAL PATTERNS
FROM LOCAL EXPERTS

ERIC NAGUSKI

STACKPOLE
BOOKS

Guilford, Connecticut

To Margaret, Izzy, and Henry. You all have encouraged and supported my love for all things fly fishing and fly tying. Without you, none of this would have ever happened. And to Virginia Naguski, who let me run feral around the trout streams of Pennsylvania as a kid. And you, Bobby Light, who stuck a fly rod in a ten-year-old kid's hands on the bank of Cedar Run . . . all this is your fault.

Published by Stackpole Books
An imprint of The Rowman & Littlefield Publishing Group, Inc.
4501 Forbes Blvd., Ste. 200
Lanham, MD 20706
www.rowman.com

Distributed by NATIONAL BOOK NETWORK

Copyright © 2021 by Eric Naguski

All photos by Mike Valla unless otherwise noted.

British Library Cataloguing in Publication Information available

Library of Congress Control Number: 2020951889

ISBN 978-0-8117-3880-4 (cloth : alk. paper)
ISBN 978-0-8117-6887-0 (electronic)

♾™ The paper used in this publication meets the minimum requirements of American National Standard for Information Sciences—Permanence of Paper for Printed Library Materials, ANSI/NISO Z39.48-1992.

CONTENTS

ACKNOWLEDGMENTS

I am offering sincere appreciation to all the anglers, fly tiers, and fly-fishing guides who made this book possible, especially Tom Baltz, Jake Villwock, Dave Rothrock, Landon Mayer, Tim Daley, Brendan Ruch, and Todd Johnson, who supplied impeccably tied flies for this book. My deepest gratitude goes to Jay Nichols, who, for whatever reason, decided I might be able to write a book.

INTRODUCTION

Pennsylvania is a cornucopia of possibilities for the fly angler. With nearly 5,000 miles of streams stocked with trout and 16,334 miles of streams that support wild trout, it's no wonder that there is some outstanding fly fishing for trout to be had in the Keystone State. There are freestone systems of all sizes. From tiny headwater streams supporting wild populations of Pennsylvania's state fish, the brook trout, to the placid limestone spring creeks of the Cumberland Valley, to sprawling tailwater fisheries like the Upper Delaware river system, the fly angler living or visiting Pennsylvania has a profusion of options that will satisfy any angler's preference for water type, angling technique, and trout species.

FREESTONE CREEKS

The Appalachian Mountains cut a swath through the middle of Pennsylvania from the southwest to the northeast of the state. This area contains most of the freestone trout streams in the state. These higher-gradient waters consist of both stocked and wild trout fisheries. Many of these streams are tiny blue-line headwaters, which eventually join forces to make up the larger freestone streams of the state. The large freestone systems like Pine Creek, which flows through the northern tier of the state, are the big-trout waters of Pennsylvania. In most other geographical areas, they would be called rivers.

Most of the state's large freestone trout streams fish well early in the season, but tend to warm during the summer months and are generally too warm to fish for trout by the time July and August come along. Penns Creek, Loyalsock Creek, and Pine Creek fall into this category. It pays the traveling angler to check local conditions before making the commitment to fish the larger freestone streams only to find that they are too warm to ethically be fished at that time of year. Each of these systems do, however, have smaller tributaries that remain cool enough to provide good fishing for the resident trout throughout the summer. As a bonus, often these larger streams are wonderful warmwater fisheries as well. They can offer spectacular fly rod opportunities for smallmouth bass and muskellunge, as well as other warmwater species.

No matter the season or size of the water, these freestone systems all provide the classic riffle-run-pool habitats where an angler can spend time nymphing classic riffle and pocket water, casting a high-floating dry fly into fishy-looking pockets, or sending long delicate casts on the smooth surface of the many picturesque glides and pools. These waters also provide many undercut banks, rock ledges, and deep pools that are effectively fished by the streamer angler.

SPRING CREEKS

Here in Pennsylvania we are fortunate to also have many limestone spring creeks that provide excellent fishing year-round. The limestone spring creeks of the central portion of the state differ from those in the south-central and eastern portions. The spring creeks like Yellow Creek, Big Fishing Creek, Spruce Creek, and Spring Creek in Centre County have a higher gradient and in many ways look like their freestone counterparts in that region. As a result, they are effectively fished using the same techniques as those used on the freestone streams.

In contrast, the spring creeks of the south-central and eastern portion of the state, like Letort Spring Run, Big Spring Creek, and Quittapahilla Creek in Lebanon County, are lower gradient and typically lack the riffle-run-pool habitats of their northern counterparts. These streams tend to be more pastoral in nature. They have fewer riffle areas and are generally slower-flowing waters, rich in aquatic vegetation. These streams are difficult (but not impossible) to fish with nymphs. In many cases the large amount of aquatic vegetation makes traditional nymphing tactics difficult, and the streams are often more effectively fished with a wet fly, streamer, dry fly, or dry-dropper combination. That is not to say that a nymph angler should shy away from these streams. As in most trout waters, nymphing can be extremely effective on these spring creeks. The numerous weed beds, deep pools, and undercut banks make streamer fishing especially effective at times in the spring creek systems.

TAILWATERS

As if the thousands of miles of freestone and limestone spring creeks were not enough, Pennsylvania anglers also have access to many tailwater fisheries. These systems vary in size from trout streams that are just a few yards wide, like Clarks Creek in Dauphin County or Pohopoco Creek in Carbon County, to sprawling rivers like the Lehigh River or the West Branch of the Delaware. As varied as Pennsylvania tailwaters are in size, they also vary drastically in flow regimes, substrates, riparian areas, trout populations, and hatches. Some are wild trout fisheries; others are stocked trout waters. Many Pennsylvania tailwaters like the aforementioned West Branch of the Delaware River look like a freestone system, with classic riffle-run-pool features.

The big bonus for anglers fishing these tailwaters is the consistent cold water they supply to the system. Most Pennsylvania tailwaters hold up all summer long: when fisheries like Penns Creek or Pine Creek in the northern tier of the state become too warm to fish responsibly, the neighboring tailwaters are doing just fine. I have found water temps in the high 50s in August on Clarks Creek—pretty amazing when other nearby freestone streams have temperatures in the 70s.

Each tailwater in Pennsylvania is unique when it comes to aquatic insects and hatches. For example, the West Branch of the Delaware has a strong dry-fly culture surrounding it. If you are a hatch-matching angler, there is no better tailwater in Pennsylvania to test your skills than on the heavily pressured wild trout of the West Branch. These fish see a lot of artificial flies, and also see a lot of insects. They are some of the toughest fish found anywhere, but if you bring your A game, you may be rewarded with a stunning wild trout from its waters. Another Pennsylvania tailwater, Tulpehocken Creek in Berks County, doesn't have as diverse insect hatches as the West Branch, but what it does have makes it a prime dry-fly stream at times throughout the year. Its enormous population of caddisflies makes it a dry-fly fishing destination in the spring, and its stable temperatures and robust midge population make it a solid choice for winter dry-fly action for those anglers that need a cold-weather dry-fly fix.

The Keystone State's tailwater trout streams are as varied as the rest of the state's trout waters. Like the freestone streams and spring creeks, they have some similarities, but they all are unique and have individual charms that make each of them worthwhile at different times of the year.

The best ways to be successful as a newcomer to any of Pennsylvania's trout streams is to obtain reliable information from a local fly shop or a good guidebook like *Keystone Fly Fishing: The Ultimate Guide to Pennsylvania's Best Water* (Headwater Books, 2017), or hire a guide to spend the day with on the water. All of these suggestions can significantly shorten the learning curve.

THE HATCHES

Pennsylvania's freestone and tailwater fisheries have aquatic insect hatches that can be truly amazing. Many of these streams have an incredible diversity of insect life, with all the major hatches of caddis, mayflies, and stoneflies represented. Not every stream has all of them, but as a region, it has the most diverse and abundant hatches. During the late spring, dry-fly anglers can find themselves in as complex and exciting hatch-matching situations here in Pennsylvania as anywhere in the world. At any one time, trout can be feeding on several species and life stages of mayflies and caddisflies, and it can be maddening and rewarding at the same time. Trout waters like Penns Creek and the Upper Delaware system are truly a dry-fly angler's paradise. But bring your A game—sometimes it's easy, but more often than not, it becomes very challenging fishing.

Aquatic insect life in the limestone creeks may not be as diverse as that on the freestone waters of the state, but the numbers of insects can be amazing. Primarily, the hatch-matching angler fishing these streams can expect to find mayfly emergences of Blue-Winged Olives, Sulphurs, and Tricos in both the central and southern streams, and Green Drakes in some of the spring creeks in the central portion of the state. The caddis consist primarily of the ubiquitous Spotted Sedges, Mottled Sedges, and some Grannoms. Midges also make up a large portion of the insect biomass in these streams and can provide excellent fishing for both the dry-fly and nymphing angler.

Terrestrial insects are important on all of the state's trout waters, and the well-prepared angler should have a selection of these land-based insects when fishing anywhere in Pennsylvania during the summer and autumn.

Baetis tricaudatus, *the Blue-Winged Olive. A ubiquitous mayfly throughout Pennsylvania's trout waters.*

THE FIFTY FLIES

In the pages that follow, you will see some old standards and some new innovations in fly tying. My goal was to put myself in the shoes of an angler new to trout fishing in the Keystone State and reach out to the busiest guides and seasoned anglers and fly tiers in the state and ask them, "What are your favorite flies?"

Many of the fifty flies featured were on everyone's list of must-haves for Pennsylvania trout fishing. Many are simple to tie, and their effectiveness far outweighs their simple construction. Some are general patterns, great searching flies on any water, while others were created for specific situations, water types, or food types that the trout key in to at certain times. There are even a few that lend themselves to specific mayfly or caddis species due to particular behaviors or prevalence in Pennsylvania waters. All fifty flies are confidence flies, and the reader can be assured that the patterns featured have earned their place on this list.

I have attempted to include as many Pennsylvania tiers and patterns as possible, but I would be remiss if I did not include fly patterns from non-Pennsylvania tiers and origins simply due to their overwhelming effectiveness on the state's trout. I hope the reader takes the list for what it is, an honest attempt to give a fly angler coming to Pennsylvania an arsenal of flies that can cover almost any trout-fishing situation they may encounter. The list is diverse, as are the trout streams of Pennsylvania. From the calm flows of the spring creeks in the Cumberland Valley to the tumbling streams of the northern tier and the technical tailwaters of the Upper Delaware system and everywhere in between, Pennsylvania has some incredible fly-fishing opportunities, and I sincerely hope that the flies listed in this volume will help anglers have success wherever they may travel throughout the Keystone State.

All fifty of the featured flies are proven to be effective in a variety of conditions throughout the year in the trout streams of Pennsylvania. Many of these patterns have come from fly tiers born and raised on the state's trout streams. They are mostly modern patterns—patterns that are producing day in and day out across the state—but I have also included some older tried-and-true flies that guides like myself and many other fanatical fly anglers in Pennsylvania use regularly with confidence. I have spoken with other guides and prominent Keystone State fly anglers about the flies featured here, and I am confident that an angler with modest skills who is a newcomer to fly fishing in Pennsylvania can be successful using the flies in this book.

In addition to the fifty featured flies, I have also made an effort to acknowledge some of the older classic fly patterns that remain effective not only in Pennsylvania but across North America. These patterns should be in every fly angler's boxes, no matter where they fish. I also want to take the time to reiterate the contributions of the state's fly anglers and tiers. To say that the sport of fly fishing has been impacted by anglers and fly tiers from Pennsylvania is a massive understatement. When you think about the giants of this sport, many of those names belong to people who call or called the Keystone State home. When you consider some of the most important contributions to fly fishing—like modern dry-fly fishing, using terrestrial insects as the basis for fly pattern design, and innovative fly-tying techniques and patterns—many of these innovations came from Pennsylvanians. Consider the groundbreaking work of Vince Marinaro, Ed Shenk, and James Leisenring. Their studies of the trout and insect life of the streams of Pennsylvania changed the way we approach fly fishing for trout forever.

The current popularity of competition-style fly fishing, tight-line nymphing, and streamer fishing affects fly concept and design. Most new flies are conceived to solve a particular problem or to be effective in catching fish in a specific circumstance. There also seems to be a continuous stream of new fly-tying products, both natural and synthetic, coming onto the market. Add to this the not-to-be-underestimated impact of social media, and you have an influx of an incredible number of new fly patterns that catch fish. It would be a daunting task indeed to try to list them all. Admittedly, many of the new patterns are derivative, as are many of the fly patterns we now consider classics. In most cases there was someone who had come before and did something very similar, which was taken by another tier and tweaked and improved upon to produce a new, different, or maybe only slightly different fly pattern.

I have tried to gather patterns to suit the dry-fly, nymphing, wet-fly, and streamer tactics most often used here in Pennsylvania. I have also included patterns that have several color and size variations so that the traveling angler can be prepared for most situations encountered in the state. Mayflies show a great amount of variation, not only between species but also within a particular species. Sometimes that variation is size; for example, the Green Drakes found on waters like Penns Creek, Big Fishing Creek, and the Little Juniata River are much larger than the Green Drakes found elsewhere. And the amount of variation found in mayfly nymphs can be astounding—many sizes and colors are represented, even in local populations. Therefore, many of the patterns included in this volume either account for these differences through the sizes recommended or can easily be altered to match local insects through a simple change in the color of the body.

As fly tiers today, we are fortunate to have a mind-boggling amount of color and material choices available. With that in mind, I have also offered color recommendations that can cover several insect species. There is no better example of this than the Rusty Spinner. This dark orange/mahogany color combination covers the spinner stage of several common mayfly species found here in Pennsylvania.

So where does one start when it comes to fly selection? I wanted to have a mix of modern and classic fly patterns for this volume. I also wanted to make sure that Pennsylvania fly tiers and anglers were well represented because, well, who knows Pennsylvania waters and their trout better than the locals? Having said that, I would be remiss if I didn't at least mention some other non-Pennsylvania fly patterns that are in most of the fly boxes of experienced Keystone State anglers and guides.

SOME CLASSIC PENNSYLVANIA FLIES

Pennsylvania has a long history of fly fishing. While many would argue for New York's Catskill region as the birthplace of fly fishing in the New World, there is a strong argument that fly fishing in North America actually started in Pennsylvania, specifically in the Pocono region of the state on historic waters such as Broadhead Creek. But I'll leave that debate for the historians to squabble over and talk about some classic fly patterns that work pretty much wherever you go. When I started thinking about writing this book, the hardest thing for me was to leave out some of the classic flies that work as well today as they did fifty, seventy-five, or even a hundred years ago.

The impact that Pennsylvania fly tiers and anglers have had on the sport of fly fishing is as significant as any other place in North America. From the likes of Thaddeus Norris, the "Father of American Fly Fishing," to modern-day fly-fishing icons like Bob Clouser, Pennsylvania has produced some of the most influential names in the history of fly fishing. A modern fly angler has to recognize the impact that Pennsylvania's fly tiers, writers, anglers, and conservationists have had in shaping all aspects of fly fishing. If you are feeling nostalgic or are the kind of fly angler that likes to revel in the history of this wonderful pastime, here, in no particular order, are ten classic Pennsylvania patterns to consider that are not covered later in this volume. I have included these particular patterns to illustrate the innovations in fly tying that have originated in Pennsylvania.

1. Vince Marinaro's Thorax Dun
2. Shenk's Minnow
3. George Harvey's Pusher Night Fly
4. Shenk's Sculpin (The Old Ugly)
5. Chauncy Lively's Carpenter Ant
6. Shenk's Cress Bug
7. Letort Cricket
8. Henryville Special
9. Leisenring's Black Gnat
10. Clouser Minnow

Vince Marinaro's Thorax Dun

To most, Marinaro's Thorax Dun is a difficult fly to tie correctly, but Tom Baltz makes it look easy. The Thorax Dun is the result of years of observation and experimentation by Vince Marinaro.

It may be said that no other Pennsylvania-based fly tier and angler changed the way modern dry-fly anglers and fly tiers look at the world of fishing with a floating fly more than Vince Marinaro. Vince's insights on fly construction and insect imitation forever changed not only the way the dry-fly angler approached fly construction but also the way the angler fishes to a surface-feeding trout. Through countless hours of observation and testing prototype fly patterns, Vince put together a life's work that has inspired and improved dry-fly fishing for all those who have followed.

Maybe no other fly better illustrates Vince's commitment to unrelenting scrutiny and practical design than his Thorax Dun. Definitely not the easiest fly to tie, when tied correctly all of its component parts come together to become the dry fly that all other dry flies tied to fool the most discriminating trout should be measured against. From its perfect mayfly silhouette to its practical elements like outrigger tails for stabilization, the Thorax Dun is the culmination of Vince's dedication to thoughtful fly tying and angling.

Shenk's Minnow

Ed Shenk's classic all-white minnow pattern is still an incredible streamer, not only for the Cumberland Valley spring creeks but anywhere trout eat other fish.

Ed Shenk knew the Letort better than anyone, period. Vince Marinaro and Charlie Fox may have gained more fame, but Ed grew up on the stream, walking its banks almost daily for decades. He ran traplines along its banks, hunted ducks there, and knew its resident trout intimately. As Joe Humphrey said about Ed, "He's the top gun. . . . Put it this way, a lot of guys talk a good game, he is the game."

Shenk's Minnow is a timeless classic streamer pattern that Ed developed over time to imitate the local forage fish. It is a fairly simple pattern to tie, composed of only two materials: marabou for the tail and a body of rabbit fur spun in a dubbing loop and trimmed to shape. Like most streamers, Shenk's Minnow can be fished with a stripping retrieve or dead-drifted.

George Harvey's Pusher Night Fly

George Harvey's Pusher Night Fly is another pattern from an iconic Pennsylvania angler and fly tier. Its flared duck breast feathers do exactly what its name implies, push water.

Want to chase big brown trout after dark? The Harvey Pusher might just be your ticket to success. Yes, I know mousing is in vogue

right now, as is throwing large streamers, but the thing that these tactics have in common is that they employ a fly that "moves water." This is exactly what George Harvey designed the Pusher to do.

I would encourage you to use a heavy tippet, no less than 10- or 12-pound test, attached to a short leader, no more than 7½ feet. The thicker tippet will prevent the Pusher from twisting your tippet. When fishing the Pusher, concentrate on areas where you think a big fish may reside. Do some daytime wading reconnaissance so you know what you are getting into after dark, and be ready to be attached to what might be your biggest trout ever.

Shenk's Sculpin (The Old Ugly)

Shenk's Sculpin, the original Pennsylvania sculpin pattern . . . still a "killer."

After Ed Shenk's recent passing, his son Stephen recalled a time when he and his dad "worked the cress" in the Letort, catching sculpins to then be photographed. Ed used these photographs to develop his sculpin pattern. He used only three materials—marabou, rabbit, and deer hair—to construct the "Old Ugly." This pattern is truly the first streamer specifically designed to imitate the ubiquitous bottom-dwelling mottled sculpin. To this day, the Old Ugly is an absolutely deadly fly, not only on the Letort but also anywhere sculpins are found.

Dead-drifting a Shenk's Sculpin along a weed bed or undercut bank is a solid tactic to elicit an eat from a big trout that recognizes an easy meal. Of course, this pattern can be retrieved with a stripping action as well. The Old Ugly remains a mainstay in many experienced anglers' arsenal of flies.

Chauncy Lively's Carpenter Ant

Chauncy Lively is a Pennsylvania treasure. His Carpenter Ant was born out of his love for fishing dry flies all around Pennsylvania but especially in its northern tier streams like Young Woman's Creek.

Chauncy Lively considered autumn the season of the Carpenter Ant. The streams of the northern tier of Pennsylvania are generally running low at that time, and the carpenter ant populations are at the highest of the year, aquatic insect hatches have waned, and the resident trout are looking for any meal they can find. More often than not, that meal comes in the form of a terrestrial insect that has somehow found its way into the currents of the stream. Fish see a lot of ants, and they recognize them as an easy meal.

Chauncy's Carpenter Ant is made of only buoyant deer hair and floats very well. It also presents the correct silhouette of an ant. Originally the pattern had the legs of the ant bound back from the head. In his book *Chauncy Lively's Fly Box*, Chauncy describes how "a talented young flytyer on the Letort" pointed out that an ant's legs originate from the thorax of the insect, not the head, and Chauncy revised the pattern in that volume to have the legs originate in the middle of the bug. Chauncy's Carpenter Ant remains in many fly boxes of Pennsylvania anglers, and it deserves a place in yours.

Shenk's Cress Bug

Once again, Ed Shenk took his knowledge of the biota of the trout stream and used it to create his Cress Bug, a fly no angler who fishes any Pennsylvania spring creek should be without.

Many Pennsylvania spring creek fly anglers consider the cress bug (sow bug) a go-to pattern for those streams. Ed Shenk was the first to develop what has served as the foundation for pretty much all modern-day cress bug patterns—a dorsoventrally flattened fly made entirely of one material, rabbit fur. Even today, Shenk's Cress Bug will fool the heavily pressured trout of Pennsylvania's spring creeks and every other trout stream in the state that has a population of cress bugs. These bugs can be found in the creeks 365 days a year and are always available to fish as a food source. I have personally witnessed trout on the Letort go head first into the weed beds, root around, and then drop back and wait for the cress bugs that they have knocked loose to come floating toward them for an easy meal.

Letort Cricket

Ed Shenk shows up again on this list with his Letort Cricket. Hard to ignore a dry fly that catches a 28-inch brown trout from the Letort.

The Letort Cricket follows the same construction as the Letort Hopper but is all black: black rabbit fur, black turkey quill wing, and black deer hair. Simple and deadly. This pattern not only can be fished dry but also be fished effectively subsurface with a split shot clamped directly in front of the head of the fly. I personally caught my first Letort trout on this pattern—a fine 18-inch fish in front

of the "Rose Bush." This terrestrial pattern successfully imitates the meadow crickets that become extremely plentiful during the late summer and early fall here in Pennsylvania. It's still a go-to fly for many Pennsylvania anglers after all these years.

Henryville Special

The Henryville Special was developed by Pocono fly tier Hiram Brobst in the 1930s to imitate the caddis he found on Broadhead Creek.

Broadhead Creek and the Henryville House have a solid place in the foundation of American fly-fishing history. Many famous anglers passed through the doors of the Henryville House and muddied their boots along the banks of the Broadhead. The Henryville Special has withstood the test of time and is still tied and sold commercially all across the country as a workhouse caddis pattern. With its body of olive floss and palmered grizzly hackle, underwing of wood duck flank, overwing of matching duck quill slips, and hackled front of the fly, the Henryville Special can be fished dead drift, skittered on the surface, or even swung like a wet fly. Any way you fish it, it remain a very effective caddis pattern.

Leisenring's Black Gnat

I would be remiss not to include at least one of James Leisenring's patterns on this list. His Black Gnat is effective as a caddis imitation during the Grannom and Chimarra caddis emergences.

James Leisenring was an innovative wet-fly angler and tier based in the Pocono region of Pennsylvania. His work in researching trout stream insects and their behavior led him to the forefront of wet-fly design, eventually evolving into the "flymph" and other soft-hackle wet-fly patterns. The Black Gnat is only one of his many, many patterns but it is a good one. It can be fished upstream dead drift, like a dry fly, or swung like a wet. Imparting the "Leisenring Lift" only adds to its appeal to the feeding trout. The Leisenring Lift presents the wet fly from upstream of the known location of a trout. The fly is allowed to drift unimpeded by drag imposed upon it by the angler until the fly is roughly four feet or so from the trout. At this point in the drift, the angler stops the rod from following the fly and the current will begin to flow against the fly line and thus "lift" the fly in the water column. As the artificial fly travels upward through the water column, increased action is coaxed out of it by the means of increased current speed and resembles more closely the behavior of the natural insect ascending to emerge from the surface of the water. This tactic can be absolutely deadly in coaxing a predatory reaction from the trout.

Clouser Minnow

Probably the most effective streamer ever created, the Clouser Minnow comes from the humble and kind Bob Clouser, a Royalton, Pennsylvania, fly tier, guide, fly shop owner, author, and mentor to many.

I think anyone would be hard-pressed to come up with a fly pattern that has caught as many different species of fish as the Clouser Minnow. Originally designed for smallmouth bass on the Susquehanna River, this fly works wherever fish eat other fish. The Clouser Minnow in its small and medium sizes works incredibly well as a trout streamer. Carry a couple in all white, olive, black, olive over white, and blue and white, and you can be assured that if you use it, sooner or later a trout will eat it.

NON-PENNSYLVANIA CLASSICS

There are, of course, many other classic trout flies that originated outside the Keystone State. Most of the flies on this list have a devoted following, and rightly so. They are time-proven patterns that will catch trout wherever you go. Also, many if not all of these patterns have spawned a number of variations using slightly different construction techniques and materials that have served generations of fly anglers. It's hard to rationalize not having at least a few of these patterns in your box when you are planning on fishing for trout anywhere in North America, not just in Pennsylvania.

1. Adams
2. Griffith's Gnat
3. Parachute-style dry fly
4. Stimulator
5. Prince Nymph

Adams

Created by Michigan fly tier Leonard Halladay in 1922, the Adams is another fly that catches trout everywhere and has spawned many variations, some of which are equally if not more effective than the original. As a young fly fisher, the Yellow-Bodied Adams was a go-to fly for the mountain freestone streams of the Pine and Kettle Creek watersheds. Tied in sizes 12 through 20, it was, and still is, a solid choice when fishing for trout in the tumbling waters of northern Pennsylvania. When the Adams is tied parachute style, it becomes a "killer" on the smooth pools and runs of many trout streams throughout the state. Add to this variation flies like the Purple Haze, which is popular in the western United States but also catches fish in the East, it's hard to argue with the effectiveness of the Adams and its many offspring.

From left to right, Prince Nymph, Stimulator, Griffith's Gnat, Adams, and parachute-style dry fly (tied by Tom Baltz). All of these patterns have proved their effectiveness anywhere trout swim.

Griffith's Gnat

The Griffith's Gnat is an easy-to-tie midge pattern that, like the Adams, was born in Michigan. It is most often attributed to George Griffith, one of the original founders of Trout Unlimited. Its inherent bugginess might be its best feature, and when tied in small sizes it works very well on midge-eating trout. It is a good option during the "warm" days of winter when we here in Pennsylvania see the largest midge emergences. The Griffth's Gnat can also be effectively fished just under the surface as well as presented as a dry fly. Its simple dressing, consisting of peacock herl and palmered grizzly hackle, often makes it one of the first midge patterns a budding fly tier ties and fishes. I know many anglers who will fish no other midge imitation.

Parachute-Style Dry Fly

There is some debate as to who developed the parachute style of wrapping hackle on a dry fly and when they did it. Many attribute it to William Avery Brush, who developed a patent for this style of fly in 1934. William Mills and Son later licensed the fly and called it the "Gyrofly." Nonetheless, this style of dry fly is just as effective today as it was back then. Many of Pennslavania's finest trout waters have long, slow pools where discerning trout have plenty of time to inspect a floating fly while deciding whether or not it is a food source. Since this is a style of winding hackle on a dry fly, not a specific pattern, the possibilities are seemingly endless when it comes to body color, wing material, and hackle color. One thing is for sure, the parachute dry fly floats flush in the surface very much like a natural mayfly, thus providing a convincing silhouette. This characteristc allows fly tiers to mimic the size and color of mayflies prevalent on their local waters.

A general selection of amber, light yellow, cream, brown, rusty brown, tan, gray, and olive in an assortment of sizes from 12 through 24 will allow an angler to cover most of the common mayflies found throughout North America. In other words, don't leave home without them. The parachute dry fly has fooled many very picky trout over the years.

Stimulator

While stoneflies do not have the impact on dry-fly fishing in Pennsylvania that they do in the western part of the United States, they are present and do get eaten by trout here in the Keystone State. The Stimulator is a classic stonefly pattern that can be used succesfully as a searching dry fly during the late spring and summer in Pennsylvania. The large Golden Stoneflies that inhabit many of the state's trout rivers are well imitated by a Stimulator. Other good places to fish this pattern in smaller sizes (#14-18) are the smaller mountain streams of the northern tier of Pennsylvania. These streams have stoneflies present, but the major factor that makes the Stimulator effective is that the native brook trout and wild brown trout that inhabit these small waters are very opportunistic feeders, and a busy Stimulator can get these fish to strike. The Stimulator also works exceptionally well as the dry fly in a dry-dropper rig.

A female Green Drake from Penns Creek—as big a mayfly as you will find in Pennsylvania. These big bugs provide some of the best opportunities of the year to land a truly large trout on a dry fly.

Prince Nymph

The Prince is one of the original attractor nymphs, its white biots serving as a trigger for a trout to feed. The Prince also serves as a good generalistic stonefly nymph pattern, best fished in heavier riffles and pocketwater in places where stonefly nymphs are found. It can be tied with or without a bead and even with a hot-spot tag or collar of orange, pink, or red. All of the aformentioned permutations work well at times. I have found that at certain times the stocked trout in some Pennsylvania trout waters are easily fooled by a fluorescent pink thread hot spot tied in behind the tails on a Prince.

The proving ground: Angler Dr. Antonio Ripepi airing it out to a distant riser. The West Branch of the Delaware River's long stretches of flat water provide more than ample time for its wild trout to inspect your offerings.

- **Hook:** #12-22 Daiichi 1180
- **Thread:** Light olive Danville's Flymaster 6/0 Nylon, Waxed
- **Post:** Fluorescent orange, fluorescent yellow, or black calf body hair
- **Abdomen:** Hare's mask
- **Thorax:** Hare's mask
- **Shuck:** Olive brown Z-Lon (⅔ body length)
- **Hackle:** Grizzly dry fly hackle

ParaNymph

(Originator and tier Tom Baltz)

If I had to pick a single dry fly to carry in my box to cover all the mayfly hatches of Pennsylvania, Tom Baltz's ParaNymph would be that fly. That's how effective this fly is. Tom created the fly in the mid-1990s and says that for a long time he didn't tie parachute flies, the reason being the influence of Vince Marinaro on the anglers and tiers of the Cumberland Valley. A parachute fly "wasn't dry enough to satisfy Vince." I suspect the fish take the ParaNymph as an emerging mayfly; however, I have seen many fish that were visibly feeding on fully emerged duns not hesitate in the least to eat a well-presented ParaNymph.

The ParaNymph has a few characteristics that make it attractive to both anglers and the trout they are pursuing. Tom ties the hackle in with the shiny side down so that the majority of the fly hangs just under the surface. The materials used in the ParaNymph also make it extremely attractive to trout. The spiky hare's mask dubbing body has movement that is consistent with an

Tom Baltz's iconic ParaNymph is a true modern-day Pennsylvania classic that works wherever trout swim.

emerging mayfly, no longer able to swim, struggling to free itself from the confines of its nymphal state. The Z-Lon shuck only adds to the fly's movement. If you take the time to watch a dun mayfly emerge from the exoskeleton of the nymph stage of development, you will see that there is movement of the insect associated with the water currents and also small shudders and convulsions made by the insect in an effort to free itself from the confines of the immature stage. The hare's mask and Z-Lon shuck effectively provide this movement. Tom says that dead flies and empty shucks on the water are shredded and "there's not a lot of grace left in there." He likes the ragged look of the Z-Lon shuck.

Another benefit of the use of hare's mask is color. Most if not all mayfly nymphs are not a uniform color but a myriad of gray, brown, tan, olive, and black hues effectively represented by a selection of hare's mask dubbing.

FISHING TECHNIQUES

Successfully fishing the ParaNymph requires a drag-free drift. A good George Harvey dry-fly leader will help the angler achieve a realistic drift with this fly, which can be fished like any other dry fly. The wing post can be tied in bright orange, yellow, or black. These wing-post color options are of great benefit to the angler. Orange is most effective in the middle of the stream in natural light and is great on bright days. The yellow posts are very effective in low light and in shady areas and are especially visible in the evenings and on streams with lots of "dark water."

Tom ties the ParaNymph with three different color posts: orange, yellow, and black. Each one works especially well in different light conditions.

On very flat water with natural light with a lot of glare, the black wing post affords greater visibility to the angler. These variations in wing-post color make the three versions of the ParaNymph relatively easy to see on the water, no matter what the light conditions may be.

The ease of seeing this pattern on the water due to wing-post color also makes the ParaNymph a great option for a dry-dropper rig. In fact, this is one of the few dry-dropper setups that I have caught a fish on both the dry and the dropper at the same time. This feat has happened numerous times, especially during the early Blue-Winged Olive emergence and the showing of the Hendricksons in the spring.

When you combine the ease of visibility, the simple but insightful construction, and the correct color and profile of the ParaNymph, it's not hard to see why this fly is so effective—and to see why Tom is one of the most heralded fly tiers and guides in Pennsylvania. It really is a must-have in any fly angler's box.

Frenchie

(Originator unknown / tier Eric Naguski)

- **Hook:** #12-20 Tiemco 450BL
- **Thread:** Red 8/0 UNI-Thread
- **Tail:** CDL hackle fibers
- **Rib:** Copper wire (small)
- **Body:** Pheasant tail fibers
- **Collar:** Peacock Ice Dub
- **Bead:** Copper slotted tungsten

When I brought up the Frenchie to Matt Kowalchuk, head guide at the Feathered Hook in Coburn, Pennsylvania, he agreed that it is a must-have. Matt fished for the US Youth Fly Fishing Team and said that for years, the Frenchie was his "confidence" fly. No matter when or where he fished, he started with this fly. The Frenchie came to the United States via the international competition circuit. Basically a simplified Pheasant Tail Nymph, the fly was championed by the French anglers and caught on with their US counterparts. It is still hard to disagree that when fishing new waters, and there are no bugs showing (or even if there are), starting with a Frenchie is a solid tactic.

In my own guiding, I carry them in sizes 12 through 18 with both standard and dyed pheasant tail. The two primary colors of

The Frenchie was welcomed with open arms by American anglers after being introduced to members of Fly Fishing Team USA by their European competitors. It is a simple fly to tie that is based on the traditional Pheasant Tail.

pheasant tail are natural and melanistic (black). Like other hot-spot nymphs, there seems to be a consensus among experienced Pennsylvania anglers and guides that it's hard to go wrong with red or orange thread for the collar. Matt says that for a long time he thought orange was best but has changed to red. Most people I know carry both. Add to the red and orange both green and pink, and I think you will have your bases covered. Bead color is a personal choice as well. I like it to match the color of the ribbing.

The Frenchie just looks like food. It resembles everything but replicates nothing—an impressionistic nymph that has that hot-spot trigger that the fish will notice and eat. It's hard to imagine a fully prepared nymph angler without a few Frenchies of different sizes and colors in their box.

FISHING TECHNIQUES

Like most other nymphs in this book, the Frenchie can be fished solo, either under an indicator or in a tight-line system, or as a dropper from the back of a dry fly. The latter rig can be very effective when you are prospecting during the summer with a terrestrial dry fly and a small Frenchie dropped off the back 8 to 12 inches. In large sizes (#10-12) the Frenchie performs very well as an anchor fly in a multi-fly tight-line rig, or it can be placed upward in the rig in smaller/lighter sizes.

This Big Fishing Creek brook trout ate a Frenchie fished as part of a tight-line rig.

- **Hook:** #12-16 Ahrex FW500
- **Thread:** Rusty brown 8/0 UNI-Thread
- **Tails:** Black Microfibetts
- **Abdomen:** Rusty Spinner turkey biot
- **Thorax:** Mahogany Hareline Superfine Dubbing
- **Wings:** J:son Realistic Mayfly Wing Material, sizes M2 or M3 burnt to shape
- **Post:** Light yellow Poly Yarn
- **Hackle:** Dark dun

Daley Dose Spinner

(Originator and tier Tim Daley)

Here's one for that fish that won't eat any other spinner in your box. The creator, Tim Daley, grew up fishing the Upper Delaware river system and knows how to feed the fly to some of the fussiest trout east of the Mississippi River. It's a flush-floating Rusty Spinner imitation that is the ace up your sleeve when you need it most.

Tim is an aquatic entomologist and aquatic biologist for the Pennsylvania Department of Environmental Protection. His knowledge of the insects and trout of the Upper Delaware system is among the best in the area. Tim flies under the radar of the more high-profile anglers of the area, preferring to satisfy his own need to fool the wary surface-feeding trout of the West Branch and Main Stem of the Delaware River for no one else but himself. His home waters are the Upper Delaware system and the Lackawanna River. Given that Tim learned to fly fish on one of the most difficult and technical trout streams in North America, it's not hard to figure out why he developed his Daley Dose Spinner.

The prolonged emergence of Hendrickson, Blue Quill, and Sulphur mayflies on the West Branch and Main Stem of the Delaware brings many anglers to ply the waters for the above-average-size brown and rainbow trout. These are among the most highly pressured and fussiest fish you will find

Tim Daley's Daley Dose Spinner, a semi-realistic mayfly spinner imitation, might just be your ace in the hole when you come across that super-picky trout. Tim's years of experience fishing over some of the most demanding trout anywhere led him to this design.

anywhere. They see a lot of spinner patterns. The spinner of the aforementioned mayflies can all be successfully imitated with a Rusty Spinner of different sizes. Tim's Daley Dose takes the typical Rusty Spinner and elevates it to a higher level—a level that will stand up to discriminating trout anywhere.

No angler should come to Pennsylvania during the spring and summer mayfly season without a full selection of Rusty Spinners. The Daley Dose should be in this selection, even if you have only a few; you might need one for that one bank-sipping fish that refuses every other spinner pattern in your box. It's not the fastest tie with the need for burning the J:son wing material, but it's well worth the time to have at least a few in your box. Tim likes to carry them in sizes 12 through 18. I find I can get away with some slightly heavier tippet, using fluorocarbon and thus preventing tippet twist, when I use this pattern.

As previously mentioned, this version of a Rusty Spinner is effective for matching Blue Quills, Hendricksons, Sulphurs, Black Quills, and even Slate Drakes and *Hexagenia* spinners. Tim's Daley Dose is well suited to the heavily pressured, flat-water situations where the fish have ample time to inspect your imitation. The way this fly lies flat on the surface in the film, combined with the translucent attributes of the J:son wings, will give the angler an advantage in fooling the most selective trout. On some of the rivers and creeks here in Pennsylvania with large populations of mayflies, such large spinner falls occur that the local trout get to see so many natural insects that fooling them into eating an imitation can

be challenging, to say the least. Tim's Daley Dose Spinner presents such a natural profile and silhouette in the water that it will provide the angler with a viable option when those snooty trout that have seen a lot of flies in their day are refusing to eat a bushier poly-wing spinner imitation.

FISHING TECHNIQUES

If the situation allows, a downstream presentation of this fly 2 to 5 feet above a rising fish is ideal to allow for a drag-free presentation. If that position is not possible, a well-placed cast just upstream of a rising trout's location, no more than 2 or 3 feet, is best. Tim recommends using as large a diameter of tippet as you can get away with. The J:son wings of this fly will twist a thin-diameter tippet at times. Remember to hesitate prior to setting the hook in this situation, allowing the fish to close down on the fly to prevent pulling the fly out of its mouth. This is sometimes more difficult than it sounds when you see a giant gaping mouth open to inhale your fly.

The Daley Dose is a fly that can save your day when fishing over super-selective rising trout. This West Branch Delaware River wild brown trout was fooled by the Daley Dose. Tim Daley photo

CDC Bubble Back Caddis

(Originator Rene Harrop / tier Eric Naguski)

- **Hook:** #14-20 Tiemco 206BL
- **Thread:** Tan 8/0 UNI-Thread
- **Shuck:** Tan Trouthunter CEN Dubbing over three wood duck fibers
- **Wing:** Two tan CDC feathers
- **Abdomen:** Tan Trouthunter CEN Dubbing
- **Legs:** Brown partridge
- **Head:** Brown Trouthunter CEN Dubbing

Rene Harrop is a true master—an icon of our noble pursuit. The CDC Bubble Back Caddis is, without a doubt, one of the best caddis emerger patterns ever developed. If you are planning to dry-fly fish any of the heavily pressured wild trout streams in Pennsylvania, bring your A game when it comes to casting, and bring the right flies. The wild trout of fisheries like the Upper Delaware system, Penns Creek, or any of the famous spring creeks see a lot of artificial flies, and they see a lot of the real thing. The aforementioned fisheries have a substantial number of long, slow pools, and the fish have plenty of time to scrutinize your offerings. If you are fortunate enough to experience a caddis emergence and the fish are rising to the adults struggling in the surface film, the CDC Bubble Back Caddis is an excellent imitation to attach to your tippet.

From the master of fooling selective trout and thoughtful dry-fly angler and tier Rene Harrop, the Bubble Back Caddis is a superb pattern to keep in your dry-fly box.

The thing about flies from House of Harrop is that they are all tied to exacting scrutiny, and they have all been developed on one of the toughest trout fisheries in the world. The CDC Bubble Back Caddis is no exception. An adult caddisfly struggling to escape the pupal shuck will ride very low in the surface film, often only its wings protruding from the surface. The Bubble Back Caddis imitates this very accurately. The natural buoyancy of the CDC keeps only the wing on the surface while the rest of the fly hangs in the surface film, just like the natural. The partridge fibers are tied in so that they extend past the wing, and any movement imparted to the fly by the angler or currents allow these fibers to move like the legs of a struggling caddis.

Another element of this fly that adds movement is the trailing shuck. The fine dubbing material, just like the partridge, moves with the current. Emergence is a harrowing time for aquatic insects: not only are they vulnerable to the fish and birds, but the seemingly simple act of escaping their silken pupal casing can be too much for some individual caddisflies and they become stuck in their own case and are crippled to the point that they are unable to fully emerge. The CDC Bubble Back Caddis is a wonderful imitation of this. The shuck and legs move in the current, but the rest of the caddis remains static. The trout see this as an easy meal and will at times even become selective to caddisflies in this state—the perfect circumstance for the Bubble Back Caddis.

FISHING TECHNIQUES

The Bubble Back Caddis is presented the same as most caddis emerger patterns, and a few options are available. Using as large a tippet diameter as you can get away with, usually 4X or smaller, a simple dead-drift presentation is often very effective, as it is with most dry flies and emergers. And similarly to most other caddis pupal imitations, if the angler can get into position to allow the fly to be pulled under the surface under direct tension, then release the tension by lowering the rod tip, the buoyant CDC wing will cause the fly to rise to the surface right in front of the target. If you can pull it off, it is a very effective presentation.

This nice West Branch Delaware River brown trout was feeding quietly along the bank when it gently sipped a size 16 tan Bubble Back Caddis.

- **Hook:** #8-18
  Tiemco 5262
- **Thread:** Tan 6/0
  UNI-Thread
- **Weight:**
  0.015-inch-
  diameter lead wire
- **Dubbing:** Hare's
  Ear Plus #1

Walt's Worm

(Originator Walt Young / tier Eric Naguski)

A sinker with a hook—that's the way Walt Young describes the original Walt's Worm in an interview with him on the podcast *Bugs and Beards*. Originally the fly was tied as an early-season anchor fly for a two-fly rig, a way to get Walt's confidence fly down in the water column. What started out as nothing more than some thread, lead wire, and hare's mask fur, Walt's Worm has become a true Pennsylvania classic fly. A staple in most guides' fly boxes, it is another simple-to-tie, amazingly effective fly. Walt made one addition to the pattern, adding some clear Antron fibers to the hare's mask dubbing for a subtle amount of flash.

Imitative of the omnipresent crane fly larvae in the trout streams of Pennsylvania, Walt's Worm is a go-to nymph for most of the guides that I know, a staple of the "guide flies." When you add a bead, it serves as one of the best anchor flies in a multi-nymph rig. Crane fly larvae are available

A Pennsylvania staple, Walt's Worm is found in the majority of the state's fly anglers' boxes. And for good reason. It may not look like much, and in truth, it is a very easy tie, but the fish absolutely love this fly.

to the trout year-round and are found in almost all sections of the stream. In larger sizes Walt's Worm can be especially effective during periods of flow increases when leaf packs are breaking up in the riffle sections of the stream. Since crane fly larvae are detritivores, they will get into these leaf packs to feed on the plant material. When flows increase, the leaf packs are broken up and the crane fly larvae are sent tumbling downstream. A large, size 8 or 10, standard Walt's Worm does a good job imitating these crane fly larvae that become available to the fish during those conditions.

FISHING TECHNIQUES

On some Pennsylvania streams such as Spring Creek in Centre County or Penns Creek, crane flies make up a large portion of the insect biomass and are available to trout pretty much year-round. Walt's Worm is effective in a wide range of sizes: I carry

Crane fly larvae are found in almost all trout streams in Pennsylvania. They range in size from a few millimeters up to 2 inches in length.

them in sizes 8 through 18. It can be fished as a single fly or as part of a multi-nymph rig, and is heavy enough to be fished tight-lined or under an indicator or as a dropper. A smaller Walt's Worm is a solid choice anytime, on the aforementioned streams or anywhere in Pennsylvania when nymphing for trout.

Roberts Drake Variant

(Originator Clarence Roberts / tier Eric Naguski)

- **March Brown Version**
- **Hook:** #10-14 Hends BL 321
- **Thread:** Pale yellow 6/0 UNI-Thread
- **Tails/shuck:** Six to eight pheasant tail fibers
- **Abdomen:** Pale tan deer hair
- **Wing post:** Lemon-gray EP Trigger Point Fibers
- **Hackle:** Brown and grizzly mixed or a cree hackle
- **Thorax:** Pale yellow Nature's Spirit Fine Natural Dubbing

The original Roberts Drake was tied by Clarence Roberts, a conservation officer from Grayling, Michigan. Initially the pattern was intended to be an imitation for the Yellow Drake. Tied in different sizes, it was utilized for any mayfly with a light-colored body. This version of the Roberts Drake has all of the same elements of the original, but the wing post is EP Trigger Point Fibers and it has a dubbed thorax, whereas the original dressing has bare thread for the thorax. Just like the original, this fly can be tied in sizes small enough to imitate the diminutive *Baetis* mayflies or big enough to be a wonderful imitation of the venerable *Hexagenia* mayflies.

As its name implies, this pattern is especially effective for the larger-profile mayflies like the Slate Drake, March Brown, Yellow Drake, Green Drake, Brown Drake, and

A Michigan classic, the Roberts Drake gets a facelift with some modern materials that give it a new life on the trout streams of Pennsylvania. It is a wonderful pattern to imitate our larger mayflies such as the Green Drakes, March Browns, Slate Drakes, and Yellow Drakes.

Golden Drake. Its large profile and good floatation make it well suited for fishing in low-light conditions, where any extra visibility is a welcome attribute. The deer hair body also makes it a good fly for heavier water that mayflies such as the March Brown like to inhabit. The long pheasant tail fibers and splayed hair on the back of the fly do a fine job of imitating a nymph shuck with good movement. This attribute, combined with the low-floating parachute hackle, also makes the Roberts Drake a viable option in slower water. I like to look for shades of deer hair that come close to matching the mayflies that I encounter on a regular basis when I am looking at deer hair in any fly shop. That way I can tie the Roberts Drake in a variety of colors to match the naturals I may see.

For Pennsylvania hatches, the Roberts Drake is my first choice for the March Brown and Slate Drake mayflies. I have been able to fool some fine wild trout from notoriously difficult waters with this fly during those hatches. Two of Pennsylvania's larger mayflies, the March Brown and Slate Drake can provide exceptional dry-fly fishing on streams such as Penns Creek, Broadhead Creek, Pine Creek, and the Delaware River, as well as many others. While these mayflies do not emerge in mass numbers all at once, they do emerge at times in numbers that are significant enough to get the fish keyed in on these large bugs. A big high-profile fly is well suited to imitate these beefy mayflies.

FISHING TECHNIQUES

A favorite tactic is to move slowly upstream casting the Roberts Drake to likely-looking water along the banks. Often during the Slate Drake and March Brown hatches the nymphs will migrate toward the banks and the fish will respond accordingly. I have found fish in surprisingly skinny water that are more than happy to eat a mayfly the size of a Slate Drake or March Brown.

Ephemera varia, *the Yellow Drake. This and other large mayflies found in Pennsylvania are particularly well suited for imitation by the Roberts Drake. The large profile and long abdomen of these mayflies is reproduced well by the "Bobby-D."*

- **Hook:** #14-16 Dohiku HDD 301
- **Thread:** Tan 12/0 Veevus
- **Shuck:** Clear Z-Lon
- **Rib:** Dark olive brown Hends Pearl Round Ribbing (fine)
- **Abdomen:** Tan Nature's Spirit Fine Natural Dubbing
- **Underwing:** Light dun CDC
- **Wing:** Natural Hareline Comparadun Hair
- **Legs:** Speckled Tan MFC Mini Centepede Legs
- **Head:** Tan Nature's Spirit Fine Natural Dubbing

Flux Caddis

(Originator and tier Eric Naguski)

Years ago on a sunny but very cold April day, I stood at the tailout of a pool on Penns Creek and watched Grannom caddisflies struggle to emerge from their pupal casing. There were hundreds if not thousands of them moving across the surface, some stuck in the surface film with their pupal casings still attached, others scurrying across the surface. It was a perfectly sunny day, and I had a clear view of what was happening around me. As I watched, it became obvious to me that the caddis were using their legs not only to swim to the surface of the water but also to move across the surface, struggling to get free. This is when I thought that the addition of some kind of conspicuous legs on a caddis pattern would be useful in imitating the movement of the legs of the emerging caddis.

The Flux Caddis came about by selecting elements from three great caddis patterns—the X-Caddis, CDC & Elk, and LaFontaine Sparkle Pupa—and adding to them to construct a versatile caddis pattern that can

The Flux Caddis is a fine representation of an emerging caddis. There are times when the trout seem to key in on the individual caddisflies struggling to free themselves from their pupal shuck. The rubber legs add movement to the fly, increasing its effectiveness.

be tied to imitate most of the caddis present in Pennsylvania trout waters. I needed something that would move in the water and finally settled on the smallest rubber legs I could find. I then added the legs to a pattern I was already messing around with that imitated the also conspicuous head of a caddisfly.

FISHING TECHNIQUES

The Flux Caddis can be fished in a variety of ways. It can be dead-drifted, skittered across the surface, fished deep below the surface if you add some split shot above the fly, or swung in the film like an emerging caddisfly. Caddisflies are ubiquitous in Pennsylvania trout waters, and this pattern covers a lot of bases. Its versatility is what makes it a great addition to any fly box. Often anglers will become frustrated during a caddis hatch. There will be fish rising all around the angler, and it is sometimes very difficult to get a fish to eat a dead-drifted

caddis dry fly. I like to treat this fly with a good floatant suitable for CDC and position myself above and across from a targeted fish; the buoyancy of the pattern allows me to drift the fly toward the fish and then a couple feet above the target. I then pull the fly under the water by having a tight-line connection to it and raise the tip of the rod, then by dropping the tip of the rod, the Flux Caddis will pop up through the surface, hopefully right in front of my target. This technique has proved itself over and over with difficult trout.

I like to have this fly in all black in size 18 through 22; all tan in size 14 through 20; tan abdomen with a brown head in size 16 and 18; all dun in size 12; rust-orange body with a tan head in size 10, 16, and 18; and olive body with a tan head in size 14 through 20. Most of the time you will see the tan and olive Spotted Sedges around, so it is good to carry at least those two colors in size 14 through 18.

Spotted Sedge. Caddisflies in the family Hydropsychidae are ubiquitous in Pennsylvania waters and can produce heavy emergences at certain times of the year.

- **Hook:** #16 Tiemco 450BL
- **Bead:** Black slotted tungsten
- **Thread:** Black 8/0 UNI-Thread
- **Body:** Black Krystal Flash
- **Wing:** Black micro pine squirrel strip
- **Collar:** Black ostrich herl

Mayer's Mini Leech

(Originator and tier Landon Mayer)

I first saw this fly when Landon Mayer and I were sitting on the bank along Penns Creek waiting for some mayflies to show (they never did that day). Landon was kind enough to pull a Mini Leech out of his box and hand it to me. I knew instantly that this fly was a good one. The pine squirrel tail moves like crazy in any current, and the ostrich herl collar pulsates with a life-like movement. Built-in movement in a fly is something I like very much—whether a trailing shuck on a dry fly or a streamer wing, movement is a trigger, no doubt about it.

I am a firm believer that you do not need a giant streamer to trigger a feeding response from a large trout. In fact, at times a large fly can have the opposite effect on a fish. Sometimes the trout shy away from a large, gaudy fly presented to them. The Mini

Mayer's Mini Leech is an incredibly buggy fly, with tons of movement from the pine squirrel strip and sized just right to be fished as a streamer or dead-drifted like a nymph. Not too big, not too small, this pattern is just right to not spook fish but still elicit a predatory response from trout of all sizes.

Leech can be used to see how the fish are going to react to a streamer on a particular day. Maybe they will be super-aggressive and chase it down when it is swung in their vicinity—that may be an indication you can indeed cut back the leader and start throwing that 6-inch articulated streamer. But at other times, the fish don't respond to something that big coming at them, and I find this especially true on heavily pressured streams or during periods of low water.

FISHING TECHNIQUES

The Mini Leech fills a niche that only a few other flies can fill. About as versatile as any subsurface fly can be, the Mini Leech can be fished like a streamer with varying retrieval speeds or dead-drifted like a nymph. From the tumbling freestone streams of Pennsylvania's northern tier to the low-gradient spring creeks of the Cumberland Valley, leeches are present at varying population densities, but most waters have them. And even if leeches are not present, the Mini Leech just looks alive, and it has the ability to trigger the predatory instinct of the trout when it sees an easy meal.

Best fished with as light a tippet as you can get away with and a mono loop knot to allow for the most movement when this fly is fished, the built-in undulations of the materials used to tie the Mini Leech make it a winner for the heavily pressured fish of most of Pennsylvania's popular trout streams. One attribute of this fly that I like the most is its small size. On our ultra-clear spring creeks that are full of structure, the

Angler Rob Incorvaia found out what was lurking under that bridge when he drifted a Mini Leech into the unknown. His smile tells it all.

small size of the Mini Leech allows an angler to present the fly to a fish directly downstream in a brush pile where the only way to get to the fish is from straight up-current to it. The unobtrusiveness of this pattern allows an angler to present a fly right into the face of a fish without spooking it. This same tactic is very useful for getting a fly under some of the low bridges common on our spring creeks. It's pretty exciting to find yourself attached to a wild trout measured in pounds that you were able to get to only because you were able to sneak a Mini Leech under that bridge.

- **Hook:** #12-18 Daiichi 1560 1XL nymph
- **Thread:** Olive brown Danville's Flymaster 6/0 Nylon, waxed
- **Bead:** Gold-plated brass or tungsten (⅛-inch on #12 hook, ⁷⁄₆₄-inch on #14 and 16 hooks, ³⁄₃₂-inch on #18 hook)
- **Ribbing:** Red UTC Ultra Wire (small)
- **Tail:** Hairs from a hare's mask (not too thick)
- **Abdomen:** Hare's mask dubbing
- **Thorax:** Hare's mask dubbing
- **Back and wing case:** Bronze Flashabou
- **Collar behind bead:** Very thinly dubbed hare's mask

Bronzeback Nymph

(Originator and tier Tom Baltz)

W hen talking to Tom Baltz about this fly, the bug nerd in me was excited to hear the story of how this pattern came about. It was after the flashback nymph patterns had been introduced, and Tom had tied some up but says that he never did very well with them. My experience was similar—the mostly opal pearlescent flash never seemed to perform for me in our Pennsylvania waters. So Tom was talking to the late Norm Shires, who kept a tank of aquatic insects for study, and Norm told him that recently some of the mayfly nymphs in his tank were swimming around "acting crazy" prior to hatching. Another thing Norm noticed (and photographed) was that these nymphs would change from a dark brown color to a bright bronze just before they emerged.

Another time-tested pattern from one of Pennsylvania's most talented fly tiers and guides, Tom Baltz's Bronzeback Nymph is an all-purpose nymph developed in the Cumberland Valley. It is a great general mayfly imitation that has just the right amount of flash to trigger an eat.

Armed with this information, Tom came up with the Bronzeback Nymph. In true Baltz fashion, the construction of the Bronzeback is such that it captures the essence of the natural insect and packages it into a form that is easy to tie, durable, and above all else, a fish catcher. The bugginess of the hare's ear dubbing combined with the trigger of the bronze Flashabou makes for an impressionistic pattern that captures the real textures and colors of an emerging mayfly nymph. Tom likes to tie and fish the Bronzeback primarily in sizes 12 and 14 but will go smaller as the season progresses and the mayflies get smaller. In the early season when the larger mayflies like the Hendricksons are around, he recommends a size 12 or 14 and then switching over to smaller flies as the season progresses. When tying the Bronzeback in different sizes, Tom recommends using sixteen to eighteen strands of Flashabou on a size 12 hook, fourteen strands on a size 14 hook, and twelve strands on size 16 and 18 hooks.

One thing that stands out for me about the Bronzeback is the color palette of the fly. While most mayfly nymphs are brownish, tannish, olivish, or black, there are some that show a great variety of colors mixed in with the base colors. Mayflies like the Hendrickson and March Brown will sometimes have yellows, golds, pinks, and white mixed in, and the bronze Flashabou will have those colors contained in its iridescent sheen. Throw in the flash of the bead, and you have a fly with built-in triggers that the fish can't help but notice.

FISHING TECHNIQUES

The Bronzeback can be fished as part of a tight-line system or under an indicator or dry fly as a dropper. This nymph "shines" wherever good populations of mayfly nymphs exist or can be used effectively as a searching pattern when traveling to new waters. Yet another scenario where the Bronzeback has been an effective pattern is during times of high, off-color water. Like other patterns discussed in this book, the Bronzeback, in larger sizes, can be an effective fish finder when conditions seem less than ideal. Areas that offer protection during high flows—like current seams, the edges of the stream and eddies along the bank, or in among the boulders—are likely places to find fish. The Bronzeback has enough flash and silhouette to get noticed in the off-color water.

Epeorus pleuralis, *Quill Gordon nymph.* *Although this mayfly seldom emerges in heavy numbers, it is present in many Pennsylvania trout waters. Tom Baltz's Bronzeback Nymph is a good representation not only of this mayfly nymph but many others as well.*

- **Rear hook:** #4 Gamakatsu B10
- **Front hook:** #2 Gamakatsu B10
- **Connection wire/bead:** 19-strand Beadalon wire, red-orange acrylic bead (6 mm)
- **Thread:** White 6/0 UNI-Thread
- **Conehead:** Copper cone (large)
- **Weight:** 0.025-inch-diameter lead wire
- **Tail:** Tan marabou
- **Body and collar dubbing:** Sulphur orange Hareline Super Fine Dry Fly Dubbing
- **Body:** Natural mallard flank and mallard flank dyed wood duck color (tan/brown)

Full Pint

(Originator Domenick Swentosky / tier Eric Naguski)

The Full Pint streamer comes from Domenick Swentosky, a central Pennsylvania–based tier, guide, and blogger. On his blog Troutbitten, Dom says that he came up with the name for the Full Pint when he noticed that the hues of the

The Full Pint streamer is the creation of prolific blogger and guide Domenick Swentosky. The amber hues and barring of the mallard flank feather feature prominently in this pattern, and it's easy to see how it got its name. Like most good streamers, the Full Pint has plenty of movement, and the addition of the conehead provides the jigging action that fish seem to find irresistible at times.

streamer he was tying blended well with those of the glass of beer he was enjoying in between flies. With no gaudy flash or sparkly rubber legs, the Full Pint encompasses a more-subtle natural palette of colors. And there are certainly times—quite often, in fact—when this strategy of more-muted colors can account for more interest from the trout than a streamer with lots of gaudy flash.

A fairly simple pattern to tie as articulated streamers go, the Full Pint utilizes only marabou, mallard flank feathers, and some superfine dubbing to produce a fly that is more than the sum of its parts. With a single articulation, and wonderful movement from the marabou and mallard flank feathers, this fly comes alive in the water. Without imitating any specific baitfish, it imitates them all. It just looks like something natural and alive in the water. With the shades of the tan marabou, the mottling effect from the barred mallard flank, and a slight shimmer from the synthetic dubbing and copper conehead, the Full Pint has the characteristics of many baitfish found in the trout streams of Pennsylvania. Like all good flies, everything tied to the hook of the Full Pint has a purpose. It's hard to go wrong with the jigging action provided by the conehead and added weight of the lead wraps on the front end of this streamer.

Baby brown trout. Brown trout are cannibalistic, and if the opportunity presents itself, a large brown trout will have no remorse about eating a smaller version of itself.

FISHING TECHNIQUES

The Full Pint is effective using a variety of retrieves under various water conditions. During cold-water periods, a dead drift or very slow jigging retrieve in deep water can trigger takes from sluggish winter fish that are holding in the deeper portions of a stream. As the season progresses, spring high water will have the fish moving to the edges of fast currents, so concentrating your efforts there with a slow to medium retrieve is a good idea. Late spring and into the summer and fall, the fish will be spread out in their summer feeding lies, so streamer fishing may be best during the low-light times of the day and even into the night. During this time, concentrating your streamer fishing around structure and the banks may pay dividends. The Full Pint is a great pattern for any time of the year.

- **Hook:** #8-14 Tiemco 5263
- **Thread:** Tan 6/0 UNI-Thread
- **Tail:** Rainbow Krystal Flash
- **Body:** Tan Ice Dub
- **Overbody:** Tan 2 mm fly foam
- **Legs:** Reddish brown Sili Legs
- **Wings:** White McFlylon

Chubby Chernobyl

(Originator Idylwilde Flies / tier Umpqua Feather Merchants)

The Chubby Chernobyl is a western foam pattern that has made its way into eastern fly boxes for good reason. The pattern is extremely useful on Pennsylvania waters, especially during the mid to late summer when we have big terrestrial hoppers, ants, beetles, and crickets available to the trout. This fly works extremely well as the dry in a dry-dropper rig, which is probably how most Pennsylvania anglers incorporate it into their arsenal. During the summer it is hard to beat a Green Weenie dropped off the back of a "Chubby" on streams like Penns Creek, Big Fishing Creek, or the Little Juniata.

The obvious features of the Chubby Chernobyl that make it so attractive to both anglers and the fish are its buoyancy, the way it rides low in the water just like a big beetle or ant, the movement of the silicone legs, and its visibility to the angler. Other than

The Chubby Chernobyl is a staple in the western United States and is also a producer here in Pennsylvania. This foam dry fly is especially effective during the late summer when fished as part of a dry-dropper rig.

tan, colors worth carrying include black, black and tan, black and purple, brown, and green. Size 10 through 14 is a good range to have for most Pennsylvania waters, but you can go larger if you are trailing a heavier nymph like a big Pat's Rubber Legs.

FISHING TECHNIQUES

Initially I was skeptical of the Chubby Chernobyl, but after having so many trout come up and try to eat a strike indicator, I figured I would give it a try. I now incorporate the Chubby into my summer fishing arsenal of flies for both guiding and my own fishing. On some streams like the Yellow Breeches and the spring creeks of the Cumberland Valley, a good combination is a small Chubby with a Zebra Midge as the dropper. A good dry-dropper rig looks like this: a 7½-foot tapered leader tapered down to 4X, a 2-foot section

of 5X tippet attached to the dry fly, and then a section of 5X or 6X tippet attached to the dropper. If you are fishing larger flies, you can upsize your tippet by one size.

This dry-dropper rig is ideally fished moving upstream, covering likely-looking water. I especially like to fish under over-hanging vegetation and along the edges of the stream, concentrating on areas close to deeper water. This is especially effective in the early mornings and on bright days when the fish will move into surprisingly shallow feeding lies, but they have the safety of deeper water close by. Do not overlook banks that have high grasses right up to the water's edge. Often there are small pockets in the bank just out of the stronger current that the fish will utilize as prime spots to lazily wait for a hapless bug to fall into the water and float right to them.

A nice pool with lots of vegetation along the banks—a good spot to explore with a Chubby Chernobyl.

Pat's Rubber Legs

(Originator Pat Bennett / tier Eric Naguski)

- **Hook:** #6-12
  Tiemco 5263 3XL
  nymph
- **Bead (optional):**
  Black Tugnsten,
  sized to hook
- **Thread:** Black 6/0
  UNI-Thread
- **Weight:** Lead wire,
  sized to hook
- **Body:** Black and
  Coffee Variegated
  Chenille, medium
- **Legs:** Black
  Spanflex or similar

Pat's Rubber Legs is the creation of Pat Bennett from Island Park, Idaho. It could have gone in the list at the beginning of the book as a pattern to have no matter where you fish for trout. But since it was included in the list of favorite flies from every single guide and angler that I spoke to about this book, I have decided to add it to the list of fifty favorites for Pennsylvania trout fishing.

Another "guide fly," the Pat's Rubber Legs is easy to tie and catches fish. When I discussed this fly with other Pennsylvania fishing guides, they often mentioned it as an anchor fly in a multi-nymph rig—and it certainly works well in the role. When you add a bead to the Pat's Rubber Legs, it will get down and stay down, enabling the nymph angler to add one or two more

Pat's Rubber Legs is one of the top-producing nymphs of all time. It can be found in most guides' nymph boxes across the USA and can be fished any time of the year in rivers and streams wherever stoneflies are found. In Pennsylvania, it is especially effective on Penns Creek, Pine Creek, and the Delaware River, as well as many other waters.

flies to really cover the water column. This rigging combo can be about as effective a prospecting nymph rig as anyone can hope for. A Pat's Rubber Legs, a mayfly nymph, and a caddis pupa or soft hackle can cover your bases when you are starting out for a day on the water, trying to figure out what the fish are going to be interested in. Early spring is prime time for this setup: mature stonefly nymphs are around, *Baetis* mayflies are hatching, and the fish may be in any part of the water column feeding on the most prevalent insect stage.

Most guides I know carry Pat's Rubber Legs in brown and black, brown and orange, yellow and brown, black, brown, tan, and yellow. These colors will cover the hues of the large stoneflies present in Pennsylvania trout streams. If you are visiting streams like Big Fishing Creek, Penns Creek, the Main Stem of the Delaware, Pine Creek, or just about any other stream in Pennsylvania, it's hard to argue against tying on a Pat's Rubber Legs to nymph some likely-looking riffles or pocketwater. If you had to choose only one stonefly nymph to have in your box, Pat's Rubber Legs would be the one.

FISHING TECHNIQUES

The Pat's Rubber Legs can be fished using a tight-line technique, under an indicator, or as a dropper under a buoyant dry fly. Fish do not seem to be especially leader shy when feeding on stoneflies or at other times when the Rubber Legs works best in Pennsylvania. Don't be afraid to use 3X fluorocarbon in

A bead added to a Pat's Rubber Legs can help get the fly down in faster or deeper water, making it a great anchor fly in a multi-nymph rig.

your nymphing rig. The heavy weight of this fly will cause you to hang up on the bottom quite often, so it's nice to have a little extra heft to your leader when trying to dislodge your fly. Remember to always check your tippet and hook after snagging bottom or some other submerged structure.

This fly works well everywhere stoneflies are found and also works as an imitation of hellgrammites and alder fly larvae. Stoneflies tend to be present in large numbers in streams with medium to large cobble and boulder substrate and some gradient to them. Here is a tip from Matt Kowalchuk, who spends most of his days guiding anglers on what I consider one of Pennsylvania's most finicky streams, Penns Creek: carry some Pat's Rubber Legs in white to imitate the molting stonefly nymphs. Good advice from someone who is out there almost every day during the season and seems to hold the keys to Penns Creek.

Iron X Caddis

(Originator and tier Tom Baltz)

- **Hook:** Dohiku HDD 301 or Daiichi #1170/1180/1100 Sizes 12-20
- **Thread:** Olive or brown Danville's Flymaster 6/0 Nylon, waxed
- **Tail:** Ginger Z-Lon
- **Body:** Roughly dubbed natural hare's mask with guard hairs
- **Underwing:** Light Dun Para Post
- **Overwing:** Natural deer hair, just a bit longer than the hook
- **Sighter:** Fluorescent orange or pink egg yarn
- **Head:** Dubbing mixture of 50/50 gray squirrel and CDC fibers, with enough Ice Dub to add a little sparkle

An X-Caddis variation from Tom Baltz, the Iron X is a top fly in Tom's dry-fly arsenal. He says it's one of his most used dry flies, and for good reason. Its buggy appearance, durability, visibility, and effectiveness make it a winner in my mind as well.

In the Cumberland Valley where Tom lives and works, the caddis start popping early and end late in the season. From early April until November, adult caddis are present on many of the trout streams flowing through Pennsylvania. The Iron X is a generic caddis pattern, meaning that Tom does not change the dubbing color to imitate specific caddisflies. Instead, he uses natural hare's mask. It is difficult to argue with this tactic, as most of the caddis we see have a tan body, and frankly, the way most caddisflies move around seemingly nonstop, body color may not matter as much as we like to think it does. Tom's use of the synthetic underwing

Tom Baltz's Iron X Caddis is a super-buggy, high-floating caddis imitation that is easily seen by anglers on all water types. It is a great fly when the trout are keyed in on adult caddis.

adds to the floatability and durability of this pattern, which works very well as a single dry fly or as the dry fly in a dry-dropper rig.

As you can see by the number of caddis patterns in this volume, the caddisfly is an incredibly important part of the Pennsylvania trout's diet in larval, pupal, and adult life stages, and having options in your fly box is important when the fish seem to have disdain for a particular pattern. Sometimes you need to change it up. It's nice to have options, and the Iron X is certainly a more-than-viable one. Its shaggy appearance only adds to its effectiveness.

FISHING TECHNIQUES

A great broken-water fly, the Iron X will float in the chop on a riffle and can be a great choice to dry-fly fish pocketwater. During prime caddis season, it can be an effective fly to pull fish from their lies in the faster water. In those habitats, fish don't have a lot of time to make up their mind whether they are going to eat a fly floating over them, and a bouncing Iron X may be just the ticket to trigger the feeding instinct of the resident trout. Tom recommends dunking the fly in a liquid floatant like Jet Fuel (I like the High N Dry).

The fluorescent egg yarn adds an extra amount of visibility to the Iron X. You can tell Tom is a full-time guide. In many of his flies, he takes into consideration the limits of inexperienced anglers' abilities and helps them overcome those obstacles through little additions to the flies. Those additions could be a design consideration, or the simple addition of a sighter. Bottom line is that Tom's flies are not just fish catchers, they are well-thought-out works of utilitarian art.

Grannom caddis from Yellow Breeches Creek. Tom Baltz's Iron X Caddis is a good imitation for one of the season's best hatches on the Breeches.

SOS

(Originator Spencer Higa / tier Eric Naguski)

- **Hook:** #10-14 Tiemco C300BL
- **Bead:** Silver Tungsten Bead, sized to hook
- **Weight:** 0.015 Lead wire
- **Thread:** Black Danville's Flymaster 6/0 Nylon, waxed
- **Tails:** Black pheasant tail fibers
- **Rib:** Silver UTC Ultra Wire (small)
- **Abdomen:** Black Danville's Flymaster 6/0 Nylon, waxed, covered with a light coat of Loon UV Flow
- **Thorax:** Black Ice Dub
- **Legs:** Black Krystal Flash
- **Wing case:** Red Holo Tinsel (large)
- **Collar:** Black Ice Dub

The SOS was created by Utah angler, guide, and fly tier Spencer Higa. I first noticed Higa's SOS in the fly bin at a Pennsylvania fly shop. The red hot spot caught my eye, and I went home that day and researched the fly a little on the internet and decided to tie a few up. I had good success with the original on streams like Spring Creek, Big Fishing Creek, Penns Creek, and Clarks Creek. The red hot spot and dark body of the SOS is really what caught my eye, and apparently it catches the eye of Pennsylvania's trout as well. As stated elsewhere in this book, red is a proven hot-spot color for us here in Pennsylvania. So many productive flies incorporate it into their construction that it simply can't be ignored when considering fly design for nymphing here in Pennsylvania.

The SOS is another impressionistic nymph that just looks like food to the trout. This

Spencer Higa's slim-profiled SOS is a nymph that gets down quickly and is well suited for tight-line nymphing applications. The red hot spot adds a little strike-inducing color and flash in this version.

Spring Creek, Centre County, Pennsylvania. This section of Spring Creek along Rock Road has been a consistent wintertime producer. Higa's SOS is solid choice for this water.

pattern really does incorporate some fish-catching traits: flash from the silver bead and rib, the sparkle of the Ice Dub, the reflective red Holo Tinsel hot spot, Krystal Flash legs, and a good mayfly nymph silhouette. All of these characteristics are rolled into one simple-to-tie nymph that has proven itself over time. The version here is similar to the one George Daniel features on his blog Livin on the Fly. His take on this fly and his specific use of the SOS during high off-color water is insightful, and I would encourage the reader to check out the post called "The 80/20 Principal to Fly Box Organization."

FISHING TECHNIQUES

The SOS is equally effective used in a tight-line rig or, the way I really like it,

as a dropper under a big foam cricket or Chubby Chernobyl. It has been a really effective summertime searching pattern for me, fished on a short dropper along the banks under tree limbs. Who knows, maybe the fish are taking it as a sunken ant. I like to fish it in the shadows of forest streams. The fish may be initially attracted by the plop of the big terrestrial pattern and then decide to eat the more diminutive nymph. Typically my dropper will be no more than 6 to 12 inches when fishing like this. Not only has this pattern proved effective during the summer, but it also has become a go-to nymph for wintertime fishing. When tied with a heavy tungsten bead, it works very well as an anchor fly in a multi-fly rig or on its own as a single nymph.

- **Thread:** White UTC 140
- **Rear hook:** #6 Ahrex Gammarus
- **Front hook:** #1 Partridge Attitude Extra
- **Shanks (from tail to front):** Three 10 mm shanks, one 10 mm shank, one 15 mm shank
- **Body:** Hen saddle palmered in front of White Chocklett's Finesse Chenille
- **Eyes:** Jungle cock nails

Feather Game Changer

(Originator Blane Chocklett / tier Brendan Ruch)

The Feather Game Changer really needs no introduction and certainly deserves its place on this list of favorite flies for Pennsylvania. I have never seen a fly that induces the instinctual feeding reaction from a fish like the Game Changer does. Any fish that eats other fish will try to eat this fly. I have witnessed brown trout chasing this fly so fast from underneath that when they eat it their momentum carries them 2 feet in the air.

The reaction to this fly from the fish is incredible. Few things in fly fishing are better than the visual aspect of the sport, and to see your light-colored Game Changer just disappear in the water because it was engulfed by an unseen fish is a truly spectacular thing. I am a die-hard dry-fly fisherman, and few things in trout fishing get me as excited as the nose of an oversize fish coming out of the water to inhale my

Both aesthetically spectacular and incredibly fishy, Blane Chocklett's Feather Game Changer is a work of art and a workhorse of a fly pattern. Another modern-day classic, this fly will catch anything that eats other fish.

dry fly. But the things I have seen fish do to a Game Changer come pretty darn close. It's all about the action of this fly. Its movement in the water screams *I'm a vulnerable baitfish*. They are time-consuming to tie, no doubt about that, but it is worth the investment. And now they are available commercially, so if you don't tie your own flies, you can purchase them.

It is difficult to think of any fly tier in recent history who has been more innovative and inspiring than Blane Chocklett. His Game Changer platform has forever changed fly tying, and the things that he and others are coming up with are not only incredible fish-catching flies, but also works of art. Here Pennsylvania fly tier and guide Brendan Ruch has tied a beautiful Feather Game Changer. Brendan works at the TCO Fly Shop in Haverford and guides for Relentless Fly Fishing Outfitters.

FISHING TECHNIQUES

The Feather Game Changer's swimming action can be manipulated by the way it is retrieved. The speed and the incorporation of rod movement affects how the fly reacts in the water. I would say that varying your retrieve until you find what the fish want is a solid strategy when using this fly. Sometimes they want it when it's moving fast, other times a slower retrieve will elicit strikes. A sharp, quick strip or series of two or three strips followed by a pause is often an effective retrieve. Change it up until the fish respond.

A selection of well-chewed-on trout-size Feather Game Changers. This fly provokes some of the most aggressive feeding behavior in trout that I have ever seen.

As far as colors go, all white, combinations of tan and white or chartreuse and white, olive, black, olive and tan, black with red Finesse Chenille, and yellow and tan are some favorites. Like most streamer fishing rigs, a relatively short leader of about 7 feet tapered down to 3X tippet is fine for most trout-fishing situations. If you are using large Feather Game Changers, you would do well to use 8- to 12-pound-test tippet. The Game Changer fishes well on a floating line or with an intermediate or sinking line. The main thing is to stay in contact with the fly at all times—you never know when the eat will come.

- **Hook:** #10-16 Daiichi 1510
- **Thread:** Camel 8/0 UNI-Thread
- **Rib:** Gold UTC Ultra Wire (small or brassie)
- **Body:** Hare's mask
- **Hackle:** Partridge

Hare's Ear Soft Hackle

(Originator unknown / tier Eric Naguski)

Not only is fishing wet flies and soft hackles a productive technique, it is just plain fun! Soft hackles can be fished upstream like a dry fly or emerger, dead-drifted like a nymph, or swung down and across. The Hare's Ear Soft Hackle serves as a great imitation of both mayflies and caddisflies present in Pennsylvania trout streams; the bugginess of the dubbing with protruding guard hairs and variations in colors of tan, brown, black, and yellow combine to look like something the trout should eat. Add a little segmentation and subtle flash from the gold wire for a trigger and movement from the mottled partridge

fibers, and you have a fly that looks like trout food.

The Hare's Ear Soft Hackle is a traditional pattern going back centuries. But no matter how old the pattern, its effectiveness has not diminished. Fishing wet flies is not as popular today as it was when I first picked up a fly rod in the 1970s. I remember seeing anglers wading in Big Pine Creek and Penns Creek fishing a brace of wet flies—and catching lots of fish, I should add—but I don't see as many anglers fishing this way anymore, not that it has gotten any less effective. And there are still anglers out there that embrace and promote the tying and fishing of soft

The Hare's Ear Soft Hackle is a time-honored classic that belongs in everyone's fly box. An easy fly to present well down and across, the Hare's Ear wet brings some absolutely vicious strikes from hungry trout.

hackles, "flymphs," and wet flies. Groups like the International Brotherhood of the Flymph continue to promote the work of Pennsylvania legends Jim Leisenring and V. S. "Pete" Hidy, whose home waters were in the Pocono region of Pennsylvania.

The effectiveness of the Hare's Ear Soft Hackle can be explained, in part, by the dubbed body's ability to capture air bubbles. This characteristic is thought to provide additional attractiveness to the trout. In an open letter to the International Society of Flymph Fishermen in 1973, Pete Hidy wrote the following: "So I speak here, for the first time, of 'mimicry flymphs' that mimic the film of air and the bubble of air that trout often see during the flymphs' metamorphosis into adult winged flies." There is little doubt that the dubbed body of the Hare's Ear Soft Hackle (or flymph) captures air and provides the iridescence of the air bubble associated with the emerging insect. Even though this pattern came a hundred years before Mr. Hidy, it was accomplishing, perhaps unknowingly to its creator, the mimicry that he refers to in his letter. There are hundreds of soft-hackle patterns out there and the Hare's Ear is just one, but it is an incredibly effective one.

FISHING TECHNIQUES

As stated earlier, the Hare's Ear Soft Hackle can be effectively fished as a mayfly or caddis imitation. Typically when fished down and across, it does a great job of imitating the fast-moving sedges as they are emerging. This pattern in sizes 14 through 18 will cover most of the caddis present in Pennsylvania. It can be fished solo or as the top fly in a tandem rig with a heavier-weight caddis pupa pattern like Tom Baltz's Deep Emerger or his Hot Head Caddis as the anchor fly.

A good technique when fishing this fly as a caddis pupa is a high-stick dead drift and then dropping your rod tip and allowing the fly to swing through the bottom of the drift. It never hurts to let the fly hang at the end of the drift as well. Adding a few slow upstream pulses with the rod tip allows the fly to move against the current and can trigger an enthusiastic strike from the trout. The Hare's Ear Soft Hackle also can be treated with a good floatant like liquid High N Dry and fished upstream dead drift like a dry fly. This can be an especially deadly tactic when the trout are eating struggling mayflies or caddis in the film.

I would encourage an angler to take the time to at least dabble in the world of the soft hackle. Swinging a Hare's Ear Soft Hackle during the early spring caddis hatches might just make you a fanatic.

Early spring on a Pennsylvania trout stream. The early-season caddis hatches are a prime time for swinging wet flies and soft hackles. The Hare's Ear Soft Hackle is hard to beat this time of year.

Charlie Boy Hopper

(Originator Charlie Craven / tier Umpqua Feather Merchants)

The Charlie Boy Hopper is a super-effective, super-easy to tie, wonderful floating terrestrial pattern that comes from Colorado-based fly shop owner and fly tier extraordinaire Charlie Craven. To a fishing guide, there is nothing better than a dry fly that consistently catches fish, is durable, and is easy for clients to see. The Charlie Boy Hopper has all of these positive attributes.

Here in Pennsylvania, terrestrial season usually starts in June as the weather warms up, and by the time August gets here, it is in full swing. The grasshoppers and crickets are a known commodity to the trout in Pennsylvania's waters. The Charlie Boy Hopper's foam and deer hair construction make it a great option for anglers wishing to fish dry flies in the summertime. Its silhouette

- **Hook:** TMC 100SP-BL #8-10, or TMC 5212 or TMC 5262 #4-8
- **Thread:** Tan 3/0 Monocord
- **"Binder" strip:** 2 by 2 mm piece of foam, color does not matter.
- **Body:** Tan 2 mm Hareline Thin Fly Foam
- **Legs:** Brown round rubber legs (medium)
- **Wing:** Natural deer hair
- **Glue:** Zap-A-Gap CA Glue

The Charlie Boy Hopper has a satisfying "plop" when it lands on the water, grabbing the attention of any trout in the vicinity. Be ready—the eat may come as soon as the fly hits the water.

is undoubtedly that of a hopper, and the distinct "plop" it makes when hitting the water is not unlike the natural and tends to draw the fish's attention when it lands on the surface.

Plenty of Pennsylvania streams have grassy banks, and they are full of grasshoppers by the middle of summer. We also have a plethora of crickets. It is a good idea to have the Charlie Boy in colors that imitate both. Effective colors for this pattern are tan, green, brown, and black. When tying this pattern in dark colors like brown and black, I would recommend adding a sighter of bright yellow foam or yarn tied in over the deer hair. This little addition makes a big difference in being able to see the fly on the water.

A wild brown trout from the George Harvey Section of Spruce Creek that couldn't resist an easy meal of a black Charlie Boy Hopper.

FISHING TECHNIQUES

Even on notoriously difficult streams like Letort Spring Run, I have seen normally wary trout move a yard or more to eat this fly. It doesn't happen often on the Letort, but I can tell you it is as exciting fishing as there is in Pennsylvania. Nothing brings about a sense of accomplishment like landing a fish on the Letort. Another good place to fish the Charlie Boy and its smaller sibling, the Baby Boy Hopper, is Spring Creek in Centre County. The trout in Spring Creek will often be in mere inches of water along the edge of the stream, and a dry-fly angler can spend many hours just stalking the edges moving at a heron's pace, spotting fish. Once a fish is spotted, accuracy and stealth become paramount. Doing your best not to line the fish, present the fly 2 or 3 feet above it and allow the fly to simply dead drift into its feeding window.

Not only is the Charlie Boy Hopper a great dry fly on its own, but it also works extremely well as the dry in a dry-dropper rig. In late summer, hang a small Zebra Midge, cress bug, or Pheasant Tail Nymph off of a Charlie Boy, and you have a deadly combo for most of the limestone spring creeks in Pennsylvania.

- **Blue Wing Olive Version**
- **Hook:** Partridge 15BNY Klinkhammer or Daiichi 1167 size 12-22
- **Thread:** Olive dun Veevus 16/0
- **Shuck:** Amber Z-Lon
- **Rib:** White Danville's Flymaster 6/0 Nylon
- **Abdomen:** Early Blue Wing Olive Jack Mickievicz Micro-Fine Blend Dry Fly Dubbing
- **Hackle:** Light dun
- **Thorax:** Ginger variant mixed with gray olive Hareline Superfine Dry Fly Dubbing

Hackle Stacker

(Originator Bob Quigley / tier Eric Naguski)

Another fly-tying style, as opposed to a specific pattern, the Hackle Stacker, created by Bob Quigley, can be adapted to a myriad of color and hook combinations to produce an extremely effective fly. The Hackle Stacker is a deadly, low-floating dry fly that imitates a struggling cripple or "stillborn" mayfly. Quigley's innovative hackling technique makes the Hackle Stacker a fly with its own unique profile and "footprint" on the water's surface. When combined with an emerger-style hook, the fly seems to really shine in heavy mayfly emergences where the fish begin to focus on the cripples and those mayflies struggling to make it out of the surface film. The hackle barbs float the anterior end of this fly, while the rest of the fly hangs in and just under the

A fly designed to ride low in the surface film, the Hackle Stacker is a solid choice when the trout are keying in on emerging mayflies.

surface. This presents what looks like an easy meal to the trout.

When discussing the Hackle Stacker with several other Pennsylvania fly-fishing guides and anglers, there was a recurring theme that this fly really seems to shine for some of the state's smaller mayflies: in the spring and fall, *Baetis* (Blue-Winged Olives), Blue Quills, and small *E. dorothea* Sulphurs. To imitate the Olives, it's wise to carry flies in sizes 18 through 22 in grayish olive and tan-olive for the spring brood and pale tan for the fall emergence. The Blue Quills are best imitated with sizes 16 and 18 in mahogany and brown with a dark dun hackle. The small Sulphurs can be sizes 16 through 22 and are best imitated with a very pale creamy yellow abdomen with a slightly darker orange to pale creamy yellow thorax and very light dun hackle. I would be remiss if I didn't say that the Hackle Stacker works well for larger mayflies as well, because it does. But they really seem to stand out as an effective pattern for our more diminutive mayflies.

The dubbing blend used here, Micro-Fine Blend, is made by Pennsylvania fly-tying material supplier Jack Mickievicz, one of first producers of prepared fly-tying dubbing back in 1968. He still owns Jack's Tackle Shop in Douglassville, Pennsylvania. In my opinion, he makes some of the finest dubbing blends for dry-fly patterns used to imitate Pennsylvania's mayflies. His Micro-Fine Blend and Poly Dry Fly Blend is spot on for our bugs here in the Keystone State.

FISHING TECHNIQUES

A standard dry-fly leader tapered down to 5X or 6X is perfect for the small mayflies often imitated with the Hackle Stacker. A drag-free drift is a must. Since they are small and ride so low in the film, these flies can be difficult to see on the water. For this reason a useful tactic is to use the Hackle Stacker as part of a tandem dry-fly rig consisting of a more visible, higher-floating dun like a Comparadun or parachute-style dun followed by a Hackle Stacker tied to a short (8 to 12 inches) section of tippet material. Not only does this setup help the angler locate their flies on the water, but the more easily seen dun pattern also can serve as a strike indicator. The Hackle Stacker is yet another fly pattern that can save the day when the trout seem to reject every other fly you send their way.

The Hackle Stacker has accounted for many fish from this section of Penns Creek that has good spring and fall Baetis *emergences.*

Baby Gonga

(Originator Charlie Craven / tier Umpqua Feather Merchants)

- **Hook:** #8 Tiemco 5262
- **Thread:** Tan 3/0 Monocord
- **Tail:** Yellow over tan marabou
- **Hackle:** Pale ginger hen saddle
- **Body:** Light yellow Ice Dub
- **Attachment:** 30-pound-test Spider Wire
- **Beads:** Two 6/0 gold
- **Eyes:** Small lead dumbbell, yellow with black pupil
- **Legs:** Gold/black Chrome Sili Legs
- **Head:** Shrimp Polar Fibre with top portion colored with jasmine Prismacolor marker; barring with sepia Prismacolor marker

While many anglers who like to throw streamers are going bigger and bigger, there is a place in the fly box for streamers that present a great baitfish silhouette and color scheme but may not be as intimidating to the fish as the same fly in a 7-inch version. Yes, those big streamers catch fish, and sometimes those fish are massive themselves, but there are other times when the fish seem to respond better to a smaller prey item. The Baby Gonga is a fly that fills that bill.

The Baby Gonga comes from the innovative, prolific, and talented Colorado fly tier Charlie Craven. When researching this book, I spoke to many Pennsylvania fly anglers and guides who like to throw streamers. The Baby Gonga was one of

A smaller streamer that pays big returns, the Baby Gonga is perfect for when the fish seem to shy away from the larger streamer patterns that many anglers are fishing these days. Show them something different.

the patterns that kept coming up. In these discussions there was a recurring theory that the sheer number of anglers throwing big articulated streamers these days has caused what can only be considered backlash from our Pennsylvania trout in some heavily pressured streams. Many people I talked to believe that, while the large streamers certainly have their place, and they obviously catch fish, presenting a smaller streamer often elicits a strike from a fish that otherwise may have shied away from a larger pattern. I can confidently say that this is often the case in the limestone spring creeks of the Cumberland Valley and during periods of low or clear water.

The design of the Baby Gonga is what makes this pattern so effective. The weight of the dumbbell eyes gets the fly down and provides a jigging action, while the single articulation and marabou tail and Polar Fibre give the fly great movement in the water.

FISHING TECHNIQUES

Like many streamers, the Baby Gonga can be presented a few different ways. It can be tied in a variety of colors, but trying to mimic the color scheme of the prey species available to the trout is a solid strategy. Olive over white, gray over white, and a baby brown trout color scheme (yellow over tan) will cover most of the forage fish found in Pennsylvania trout streams.

During the cold-weather months, while fishing streams like Penns Creek or Pine Creek in the northern tier of Pennsylvania, concentrating on deep water is a good idea. Utilizing a sinking line or a sinking tip like

A 14-inch Spring Creek brown trout who decided that a 6-inch brown trout would make a nice midwinter meal. The Baby Gonga does a great job of impersonating a young brown trout.

a RIO Trout VersiLeader and a slow jigging or crawling retrieve can get those lethargic wintertime trout to move for your Baby Gonga. The post-spawn fish are hungry, but cold, and sometimes as slow a retrieve as you can possibly do is what they will take. During the rest of the year, I would suggest putting the Baby Gonga where the baitfish are. Stream banks, structure, and likely ambush points like undercut banks and midstream boulders are always likely spots to find a fish willing to chase a streamer.

Rigging the Baby Gonga is similar to rigging most other streamers: the fly is attached with a nonslip mono loop knot, and a simple leader with as heavy a tippet as you can get away with is ideal. Fluorocarbon is a good idea due to its abrasion resistance. Let's face it—when you are throwing streamers you may find yourself attached to the trout of a lifetime, and when it's headed for a brush pile or boulder, it's nice to be able to "put the wood" to a big fish. Your tackle should be up for the task.

CDC Loopwing Emerger

(Originator and tier Eric Naguski)

This CDC Loopwing Emerger has its roots in the late Shane Stalcup's emerger pattern, but instead of imitating an entire emerging dun, this fly combines both the nymph and the dun life stages of a mayfly. The rear portion of the fly is an entire nymph with tails, abdomen, legs, and thorax, and it then transitions into the thorax and head of the adult insect. The CDC loop wing floats in the surface film and allows the slightly weighted rear portion of the fly to ride just below the surface. The ragged rear portion of the fly has some movement

- **Hendrickson Version**
- **Hook:** #12 Daiichi 1167 Klinkhammer
- **Thread:** Olive dun Veevus 14/0
- **Tail:** Wood duck flank
- **Abdomen:** Dark brown SLF Squirrel Dubbing
- **Rib:** Black UTC Ultra Wire (medium)
- **Legs:** Wood duck flank
- **Thorax:** Dark brown SLF Squirrel Dubbing
- **Wing:** Medium dun CDC
- **Hackle:** Medium brown dun
- **Thorax:** Pink Cahill Nature's Spirit Fine Natural Dubbing
- **Head:** Hendrickson Nature's Spirit Fine Natural Dubbing

A transitional dry fly, the CDC Loopwing Emerger is part nymph, part dun mayfly. Riding low in the surface film with good movement from the buggy nymph dubbing and tails, this pattern works well for all mayflies found in Pennsylvania.

courtesy of the spiky squirrel dubbing and wood duck flank legs.

Most mayfly nymphs are darkly colored, and often the emerging dun is a lighter color—this is especially true in many of Pennsylvania's major hatches of Hendricksons, Sulphurs, and *Drunella* mayflies. This characteristic is incorporated into the design of this fly, which mimics the contrasting colors of the emerging dun and nymph. In addition, as the dun emerges from the nymphal shuck, it struggles to free itself from the confines of its former life stage. This movement is mimicked in this fly through the use of the spiky, picked-out dubbing. The low-floating profile and realistic structure make the CDC Loopwing Emerger a go-to pattern for any mayfly species that hatches midstream. It has proven itself to be a great pattern on Pennsylvania trout streams for Hendricksons, Blue Quills, Blue-Winged Olives, Sulphurs, or even Green Drakes when tied in larger sizes.

FISHING TECHNIQUES

To present this fly effectively, the cast should put the fly 2 to 4 feet above the targeted rising fish. A simple dead-drift presentation usually is all that is needed to feed a trout that is keyed in on emerging mayflies. Applying some floatant on just the front half of the fly will help it remain in the surface film.

To imitate mayflies other than the Hendrickson, which is shown here, you can

A Penns Creek resident brown trout that was sipping emerging Hendricksons along the bank was a pushover for the CDC Loopwing Emerger.

adjust the hook size and the color of the dubbing and hackle used for the front portion of the fly. The CDC Loopwing Emerger has also been an ace in the hole for the Large Blue-Winged Olives (*Drunella cornuta* and *Drunella tuberculata*) on Penns Creek and Pine Creek. The fish seem to get ultra-selective during this hatch and focus on the emerging insects or cripples. When they are eating the emergers, this fly has been a good one.

This pattern fishes best using a nonslip mono loop knot and as fine a tippet as you can practically use. It takes some practice to tie a small nonslip mono loop knot, but the extra movement it affords can be beneficial.

Dead Ringer Caddis

(Originator and tier Jake Villwock)

- **Hook:** #14-16 Orvis Czech Nymph
- **Thread:** Camel 6/0 UNI-Thread
- **Abdomen:** Olive SLF Bug Dub
- **Shell back:** Natural pheasant tail
- **Thorax:** Brown SLF Bug Dub
- **Wing pads:** Black Life Flex
- **Horns:** Lemon barred wood duck
- **Weight:** 0.010-inch-diameter lead wire

Pretty much every single trout stream in Pennsylvania has a population of caddisflies. Some have more than others, but they all have them. Unlike mayflies, caddisflies go through complete metamorphosis: egg, larva, pupa, adult. It would be hard to imagine a fully competent fly fisher not having every stage of the caddis life cycle covered. We even add the eggs to some of our flies.

Caddis emergences can be frustrating to fish at times. The adults are everywhere in the air, and we see trout splashing on the surface. So with high anticipation we attach an adult caddis pattern to our tippet and eagerly cast to a fish that has been rising every twenty seconds since we first saw him. Perfect cast, perfect drift right over our target, and . . . nothing. OK, do it again. Again nothing. OK, pick up the fly to cast again. The fish rises again, throwing water a foot and a half in the air. Again the fish ignores our offering . . . Most fly anglers who have been around enough have encountered this scenario. Often the trout are keyed in on the fast-swimming caddis pupae that are heading to the surface to emerge. This can explain why the fish are ignoring our adult caddis imitations that are the right size and color to match the naturals.

Relentless Fly Fishing's Jake Villwock has come up with a fly with a name that pretty much sums up what it is. The Dead Ringer Caddis is an excellent caddis pupa pattern, effective wherever caddisflies are found.

The Dead Ringer Caddis comes from Pennsylvania fly tier, guide, and outfitter Jake Villwock. It is a caddis pupa pattern that captures the conspicuous anatomical features of the natural. Caddis pupae use their strong swimming legs to reach the surface of the water. When pupae are swimming, their antennae are oriented toward the rear of the body; the wings, not fully functional, are held at the sides of the thorax and abdomen. The Dead Ringer's construction incorporates the morphological features of the caddisfly pupa and makes for an excellent imitation of the emerging pupa, but remains fairly simple to tie.

Breaking the fly down, you can see why it is so effective. The SLF Bug Dub uses a combination of synthetic and natural fibers with some rabbit guard hairs left in. The SLF's "bugginess" captures air bubbles, and the synthetic fibers and subtle flash provide some glint of light reflection, very similar to what the gasses expelled by the living caddis pupae do when they are swimming to the surface and separating from the pupal casing. The dark dorsal stripe provided by the pheasant tail fibers is very similar to the dark dorsal portion found in many of the common caddisflies present in Pennsylvania waters, especially the Spotted Sedges (Hydropsychidae). The contrast between the abdominal and thoracic coloration of the natural insect is mimicked by the contrasting colors of dubbing Villwock has chosen to use for this fly's abdomen and thorax. The "wing pads" of the imitation do a good job of representing the wings of the natural, and the swimming legs are successfully incorporated into the fly through the use of the Life Flex material. And last, but not least, the posterior-facing antennae are incorporated into the fly through the use of two lemon wood duck flank barbs. So when you combine all of these parts of the constructed fly, you come up with what amounts to a "dead ringer" for the natural.

FISHING TECHNIQUES

The Dead Ringer can be fished dead drift like a nymph, swung like a wet fly, or if you add a good amount of floatant to the fly, presented in the surface film like an emerger/dry fly. A fairly simple tie, Jake's Dead Ringer Caddis is a pupa pattern worth having in your caddis box, especially when fishing Pennsylvania trout fisheries like the Lackawanna River, Tulpehocken Creek, the Main Stem of the Delaware, the Lehigh River, or any other water that has a high population of caddisflies.

*Caddis pupae can occur in incredibly large numbers. Here, Speckled Sedge (*Neophylax sp.*) pupal cases cover a rock from Penns Creek. Fishing pupal imitations during caddis emergences are often the only way to be consistently successful when the trout are feeding on the ascending caddis pupae.*

Blow Torch

(Originator Devin Olsen / tier Eric Naguski)

- **Hook:** #12-16 jig hook
- **Thread:** Fluorescent orange Veevus 16/0
- **Bead:** Copper bead, sized to hook
- **Weight:** 0.015-inch-diameter lead wire
- **Tag:** Three strands Glo-Bright #5
- **Over ribbing:** 5X tippet material
- **Under ribbing:** Opal Mirage Micro Flashabou
- **Abdomen:** Peacock black Ice Dub
- **Collar:** Mottled tan hen hackle
- **Hot spot:** Fluorescent orange Veevus 16/0

From competitive angler Devin Olsen comes the versatile and super-fishy Blow Torch, which has its roots in a Czech chub fly. Hot spots on flies are not new to fly design—one can go back to Theodore Gordon's Bumblepuppy to see a hot spot in action—and tag nymphs have been popular in Europe for a while as well. When I was discussing nymphs with Pennsylvania anglers and guides, a hot spot seemed to be a part of many of the fly patterns that came up. And the Blow Torch is no exception—in fact, it has two.

Most of the anglers I spoke to use the Blow Torch in size 14 or 16 here in Pennsylvania. The trout certainly do seem to notice it. The contrast between the bright tag and collar hot spots and the dark dubbing combined with the movement of the soft-hackle collar make the Blow Torch an effective fly in all water types. The collar's pulsating action adds to its attraction, so even in slow currents this fly has an inherent action that

All of the components of a buggy attractor nymph are incorporated in Devin Olsen's ultra-effective Blow Torch.

can trigger a response from a fish. Like other nymphs in this list of fifty flies, the contrast between dark and bright flashy materials is a proven fish-catching combination. In off-color water it pays to have a few Blow Torches with a pink tag and collar instead of orange in your box.

FISHING TECHNIQUES

The Blow Torch seems to be especially effective just before a mayfly emergence. When fished in tandem with another nymph with more natural coloration, it enhances your chances of pulling a fish from its lie to eat your fly. It could be the flash of the dubbing and bright color of the hot spots that initially grab the attention of the fish and then the fish eats the other nymph, but whatever the reason, the combination seems to produce more fish than either nymph fished alone. With a bead and some lead wire wraps, it can be used as a point fly in a multi-nymph setup. Like most of the nymph patterns in this book, the Blow Torch can be fished under an indicator, tight-lined, or as part of a dry-dropper rig.

Section of good nymphing water from a central Pennsylvania stream. Nymphing anglers could do well in a spot like this with a Blow Torch incorporated into their nymphing rig.

- **Hook:** #12-14 Partridge CZ Patriot Czech Nymph
- **Thread:** Pink Veevus 6/0
- **Bead:** Pink slotted tungsten (3.3 mm)
- **Body:** Pink Caster's Squirmito

Squirmy Worm

(Originator unknown / tier Eric Naguski)

All the anglers I look up to fish worms." That's how Matt Kowalchuk responded when I said I was going to put "the worm" in this book. There seems to be two distinct groups of anglers when it comes to the Squirmy Worm: they either embrace the effectiveness of the worm or they disdain it and refuse to even acknowledge it as a fly. There was even an attempt to ban the Squirmy in the competitive arena. I will leave that argument there. I was among those who held the worm in contempt, but my mind has been changed and I am now a proponent, mainly because I am a proponent of people catching fish on a fly rod. Could be because I get paid for it . . .

The history behind the Squirmy Worm is sketchy, with most references going to Dave Hise of North Carolina as the creator, but I have not been able to officially confirm that. All I know for sure, as a fishing guide, is that this fly catches fish, *everywhere*. It has saved the day for me more than once, and just when you think it's impossible that another fish could come from that spot you've already caught several fish from, you tie on the worm and bam, there's another fish. I'm not talking about just stocked fish either (although the stocked rainbows seem particularly fond of the thing). The wildest brown trout on the toughest spring creeks seem to find the fly just too appealing to

Like it or not, the Squirmy Worm is a fish catcher. The movement and color of "the worm" seem to be almost irresistible to trout.

pass up at times. When the struggle is real, and believe me some days it is very real, the worm will produce when nothing else will.

FISHING TECHNIQUES

Everyone should realize that aquatic worms are a large proportion of the macroinvertebrate community in most streams. And not only this, but during periods of high water when our streams run bank full or even over their banks, earthworms are dislodged from eroding banks. So there is some science here, folks. Fish eat worms. These periods of high, dirty water are a great time to fish the Squirmy Worm. A Squirmy fished in the soft edges of faster currents and along grassy banks can produce when nothing else will.

Good colors to have are pink, red, and tan. The Squirmy can be fished under an indicator or in a tight-line rig. For anglers wishing to learn how to tight-line nymph, I think the Squirmy is a great fly to start with. It is heavy enough that it will get down and create a direct connection with the angler, and if you take this rig to a stocked stream, chances are you are going to get a fish to eat the fly. So a new tight-line nympher can really get a feel for what a strike looks like. I say embrace the worm, have some fun, and go catch some fish.

Relentless Fly Fishing guide Neil Sunday helps bring a fish to net for a client on the Allenberry section of the Yellow Breeches. Heavily stocked streams like the Yellow Breeches are a fine place to drift a Squirmy.

Hook: #12-18
Tiemco 230BL
Thread: Gray 8/0
UNI-Thread
Weight:
0.025-inch-
diameter lead wire
Dubbing: Sow bug
Sow-Scud Dubbing
Dorsal line: Loon
UV Flow

- **Hook:** #12-20 Tiemco 100BL
- **Thread:** Tan 8/0 UNI-Thread
- **Shuck and overbody:** White/clear Hi-Vis Antron Fiber
- **Underbody:** Rhyacophila Blue Ribbon Flies Zelon Dubbing
- **Wing:** Deer hair
- **Head:** Tan Hareline Superfine Dubbing

LaFontaine Emergent Sparkle Pupa

(Originator Gary LaFontaine / tier Eric Naguski)

(Originator and tier Jake Villwock)

One of the most innovative and insightful fly tiers, fly-fishing entomologists, and fly anglers of the twentieth century, Gary LaFontaine's contribution to fly fishing is difficult to overstate. His groundbreaking book *Caddisflies* provided a never-before seen look into the biology and behavior of caddisflies. Arguably one of the most persistent benefits to come out of Gary's work is the LaFontaine Emergent Sparkle Pupa. What is now a classic to most patterns, cean. This dark line is faithfully reproduced

the Emergent Sparkle Pupa and its kin the Deep Sparkle Pupa are staples in most experienced fly anglers' boxes through the use of LaFontaine. This pattern has a few features that allow it to stand out. First is Gary's innovative use of Sparkle Yarn to replicate the gas bubble formed in the caddis pupa cocoon as it emerges. This bubble can catch the light that creates a "sparkle" that the trout see and react to. In addition to the trigger of the Sparkle Yarn, the movement of the shuck the sow bugs in the Cumberland Valley are

Gary LaFontaine put years of science and observation behind his fly patterns. The Emergent Sparkle Pupa is just one example of this. The bubble effect created by the Antron overbody is what makes this fly so special. (sow bug) pattern that every spring creek angler should carry.

of the Emergent Sparkle Pupa is an added feature that can coax a picky trout into coming to your fly.

FISHING TECHNIQUES

As with many of the patterns in this book, the Emergent Sparkle Pupa can be presented a few different ways. A standard dead-drift presentation can be very effective when casting to fish feeding consistently on caddisflies in or just below the surface. Caddis emergences are notoriously frustrating for fly anglers, when there are hundreds if not thousands of them in the air and fish are throwing water a foot into the air as they slash through the surface of the water, and yet they ignore the perfectly presented dry fly. This is a situation where the Emergent Sparkle Pupa can improve your chances of success.

An angler can try a couple different presentations in this situation. First, using no floatant, gently massage water into the fly prior to casting; this will allow the fly to sink just slightly. Then, using a dead-drift presentation, present the fly to the trout just below the surface. Another option is to add a very small split shot about 8 inches above the fly, present the fly from upstream of the fish, and allow the fly to sink as it drifts toward it. A couple feet before the fly arrives at the target, keeping

If you really want to up your game, try sight-fishing a single SYE Sow Bug to a

LaFontaine's Deep Sparkle Pupa can be fished in a multi-fly rig with the Emergent Sparkle Pupa. This is a good tactic to determine where in the water column the fish are feeding.

a somewhat tight connection to the fly, lift the rod tip, causing the fly to rise in the water column. If done properly, this presentation can imitate a caddis pupa swimming toward the surface and entice the fish to chase it down.

Yet another presentation option is to hang the Emergent Sparkle Pupa off the back of a dry fly as a dropper. This tactic often makes strike detection a little easier when the fish are feeding just below the surface. Fishing the Emergent Sparkle Pupa in tandem with a Deep Sparkle Pupa also can increase your chances of fooling a caddis munching trout. For Pennsylvania waters a good selection of the Emergent Sparkle Pupa is tan, olive, black, and bright green in sizes 14 through 20. The SYE Sow Bug is a fly that can make those kinds of memories happen.

Extended Body Drake

(Originator unknown / tier Eric Naguski)

- **Green Drake Version**
- **Hook:** #8-12 Daiichi 1160 or Daiichi 1167
- **Thread:** Yellow 6/0 UNI-Thread
- **Tails:** Dark moose mane fibers
- **Rib:** Yellow 6/0 UNI-Thread
- **Abdomen:** Two thin pieces of white 2 mm foam colored with a cream Prismacolor marker
- **Thorax:** Pale Morning Dun Hareline Superfine Dubbing
- **Wing:** Dyed chartreuse deer body hair
- **Hackle:** Grizzly dyed olive Whiting Dry Fly Hackle

Every year anxious fly anglers await the arrival of the Green Drake (*Ephemera guttulata*). The emergence of these massive mayflies is an event that many Pennsylvania anglers plan their summer vacations around. The spectacle that is the Green Drake hatch brings hordes of anglers to streams like Penns Creek in late May every year. It truly is a spectacle, and even if you hate to fish with a crowd, it should be witnessed at least once in every fly angler's lifetime. Several other Pennsylvania streams have Green Drake populations, but few if any have drakes in the numbers and especially the large sizes that occur on Penns Creek. Most of the mayflies are a size bigger on Penns Creek than on any other Pennsylvania stream, and the Green Drakes are no exception.

The foam body and correct profile of the Extended Body Drake is a comfort when an angler is fishing in the low-light hours that are often the time of day that hosts the heaviest drake emergences.

An issue that must be confronted when tying dry flies this large is not only finding hooks big enough but also designing a fly that is durable and will actually float. I tie this pattern on a size 8 Daiichi Klinkhammer hook, and overall the fly is close to 2 inches long to match the female duns on Penns Creek. The males are a size smaller. The use of foam for the abdomen and incorporating a hook that is not too heavy make floating this large fly a non-issue. It also makes using a heavier rod unnecessary to cast this fly. I typically use a standard 9-foot 5-weight rod for my drake fishing, and it works just fine with this big fly. The deer hair wing provides a great silhouette and color for the greenish tinted wings of the natural. And thanks to modern genetic dry-fly hackle, finding a hackle with long stiff barbs is easy too. Overall this fly is relatively easy to tie and takes only a little time to construct the abdomen. I typically will tie a bunch of abdomens ahead of time so they are ready when I sit down to tie the complete fly.

The Green Drake emergence can happen all day long, with duns trickling off during the daytime, but after nightfall the number of duns emerging often will increase dramatically. Having a fly that you know is floating is a nice thing when you are fishing well into the night.

FISHING TECHNIQUES

When it comes to fishing this fly, forget the long, fine dry-fly leaders. A simple 7½-foot leader that tapers down to 1X or 2X and then a 2-foot section of 3X tippet is my standard Penns Creek Green Drake dry-fly leader. At night I will go shorter and heavier. My leader for other streams where the flies are not as large as they are on Penns will be similar in length but lighter.

Nighttime tactics with this pattern are pretty simple. I try to keep my casts as short as possible and usually employ a dead-drift presentation. When there are a lot of naturals on the water, a little wiggle of the rod tip to introduce some movement into the fly helps your offering stand out among the others. While fishing during the day, I find that imparting some movement to my presentation can make a huge difference in how the fish react to my fly. I like to move slowly, looking for feeding fish. Many times the fish will ignore still duns drifting overhead, rising only to the duns that are struggling on the surface.

Tactics are pretty much the same for streams other than Penns—I just use a smaller fly. I carry this fly in sizes 8 through 12, and I also carry a coffin fly of similar design. It has a white abdomen, a thorax of black dry-fly dubbing, spent grizzly hackle tips for wings, and a white post of EP Trigger Point Fibers with grizzly hackle. This general style of extended body foam abdomen and deer hair parachute post works well for the late Hex (*Hexagenia atrocaudata*) found on streams like the Yellow Breeches in late summer. The late Hex version has pale yellow foam on the bottom and brown foam on top of the abdomen with a dark honey-colored thorax, natural deer hair post, and medium Pardo coq de leon hackle wound around the post.

Roamer

(Originator and tier Jake Villwock)

- **Hook:** #2/0 Partridge Universal Predator
- **Thread:** Fluorescent Green Danville Flymaster Plus 210
- **Keel:** 0.025-inch-diameter lead wire
- **Tail:** Grizzly rooster cape over natural bucktail
- **Flash:** Pearl Flashabou
- **Rear body:** Natural bucktail
- **Rear back:** Minnow belly Senyo's Laser Dub
- **Mid body:** Pearl UV Polar Chenille
- **Front body:** Natural bucktail
- **Throat:** Red Krystal Flash
- **Pectoral fins:** Grizzly hen saddle
- **Overwing:** Dyed gray peacock herl
- **Head:** Minnow belly over white Senyo's Laser Dub

The Roamer, guide and outfitter Jake Villwock's signature fly, is not only a smallmouth bass fly, but in reality will work for any piscivorous fish that swims. It's easy to understand the addictive nature of fishing streamers for trout. When conditions permit, it's hard to beat the visual of a big brown trout tracking your streamer through the water, seeing the glowing white inside of its mouth as it inhales your fly. So like all good flies, everything wrapped on the hook of the Roamer is there for a reason. Two main reasons: profile and movement.

Not just a smallmouth bass fly, the Roamer will catch any predatory fish that swims. It is an excellent imitation of our native fallfish and other full-bodied forage fish found in Pennsylvania's trout waters.

Jake developed the Roamer when fishing for striped bass with his dad. His dad was doing very well fishing a soft plastic lure called a fluke. Jake had the fly rod and was not catching the fish that his dad was with the fluke rig, so he set out to design a fly that had the fish-catching action of the fluke. The large head of the Roamer does a great job of moving water, causing the rear of the fly to kick around when retrieved with a sharp start-and-stop strip. This action is appealing to any fish that feeds on baitfish. A wounded baitfish is easy pickings for a predator, and the erratic movements of an injured baitfish can entice any fish to strike.

The Roamer proved itself to me as trout streamer on the notoriously difficult fish of the Lower West Branch of the Delaware River. One year during the Friends of the Upper Delaware River (FUDR) annual One Bug Tournament, we were met with sleet, snow, freezing rain, rain, and general nastiness. I chose to fish the Roamer as my one bug the first day of the tournament. It didn't matter that the water temps were in the mid-40s, the fish jumped on a gray-over-white Roamer fished with a slow but severe strip with a short jerk of the rod tip. I was in the back of the boat fishing areas the person in the front had already fished with another streamer. The Roamer got many more follows, strikes, and fish than the other streamer. I don't think it was the angler either—I was throwing the Roamer into the same areas and getting different results.

FISHING TECHNIQUES

The movement of the back two-thirds of the Roamer is such that even if the fly is retrieved at a steady rate, the feathers and bucktail pulsate back and forth on a horizontal plane with the hook and head of the fly, mimicking a slow-swimming baitfish. This action adds another dimension to the Roamer. It is best fished in most trout situations on a leader no longer than 7½ feet and seldom lighter than 2X tippet. In smaller sizes (size 1 or 2 hook) you can use a slightly lighter tippet. Jake likes to use a 6-foot leader and 0X to 2X tippet attached by a swivel to the leader.

A good tactic is to fish the Roamer around structure. Boulders and woody debris are always good choices, especially where currents are funneled through or around them. In addition, undercut banks can also be prime lies for a brown trout waiting to ambush an unsuspecting baitfish as it passes by. It's a good idea to have a few Roamers in gray and white, olive and white, all white, and chartreuse and white in your arsenal of streamers. Remember, they are not just for smallmouth bass.

- **Blue Winged Olive Version**
- **Hook:** #8-22 Tiemco 100 or 100BL
- **Thread:** Dark olive Danville's Flymaster 6/0 Nylon, waxed
- **Tails:** Medium Pardo coq de leon
- **Abdomen:** Fur dubbing made of a mix of muskrat, olive rabbit fur, and rusty Australian opossum
- **Thorax:** Fur dubbing made of a mix of muskrat, olive rabbit fur, and rusty Australian opossum
- **Wing:** Dun CDC

CDC Comparadun Variant

(Originator unknown / tier Tom Baltz)

Talk about a workhorse of a dry fly for Pennsylvania waters. The Comparadun is a great pattern that has its roots in Fran Betters's Adirondack pattern the Haystack, but it was refined and then popularized by Al Caucci and Bob Nastasi in their groundbreaking book *Hatches*. In that book Al states that he was fishing the fly in the 1960s. I do know that Al and Bob did a lot of fishing and research in Pennsylvania leading up to the publication of the book in 1975, so I like to think of the Comparadun as a Pennsylvania fly. Maybe it's revisionist

history, and feel free to set me straight when you see me, as I do tend to get a bit romantic about fly fishing and fly tying here in Pennsylvania. Anyway, no matter where it was first tied and fished, it remains one of the best dry flies ever created.

As a platform, the basic Comparadun structure of split tails, dubbing, and a deer hair wing allows the creative and observant fly tier the ability to develop color combinations that are specific to mayflies of their home waters. And with the ability to research photos of mayflies from all over

Delicate yet durable, this Tom Baltz–tied CDC Comparadun is in a BWO theme. This pattern is a must-have for any dry-fly angler hoping to fool the most "educated" trout swimming in Pennsylvania trout waters.

the world, the possibilities are endless when it comes to specific color combinations and sizes of the Comparadun.

There are a few choices for wings other than deer hair for the Comparadun. CDC works especially well on smaller flies. Snowshoe hare is another great choice, as it floats extremely well but does not require the maintenance of CDC. And if you can find some good-quality elk hair, it makes a really nice-floating Comparadun wing. Fly tiers are now incorporating new materials like EP Trigger Point Fibers into their Comparadun patterns. Any good dry-fly dubbing will work for the body and thorax; Caucci and Nastasi had their original spectrumized fur blends to match specific mayflies, and many anglers I know blend their own dubbings to match the local mayflies. The wing of the Comparadun and its split tails that serve as outriggers allow the fly to float extremely well, yet right in the surface film.

This fly was created for picky trout and has withstood the test of time on some of the most difficult and technical dry-fly waters in Pennsylvania.

FISHING TECHNIQUES

When presenting the Comparadun, typically the angler has located a rising fish. Getting into good position is critical. If you can do so without spooking the fish, positioning yourself upstream above the fish at an angle makes for the easiest drag-free presentation most times. And here is where it pays to learn and master the reach cast. A good reach cast will put the fly in the fish's feeding lane in a manner that it will arrive to the fish fly-first, hopefully preventing any

portion of the leader or tippet from being pulled downstream, creating drag. Drag is the enemy here. I hear anglers talk about micro drag, but really drag is drag, no matter how severe it is. Like Tom Baltz once said to me, "Drag is like pregnancy—you are either pregnant or you aren't. Your presentation is either drag-free or it's not—there is no in between." Admittedly there are times when a little movement of the dry fly can induce a positive response from the fish, but the majority of the time, especially when the fish are eating mayflies, drag is a very bad thing.

To cover most of the major Pennsylvania mayflies, a good Comparadun selection would be as follows: size 18 and 20 olive for BWO mayflies, size 16 and 18 mahogany for Blue Quills, size 14 mahogany for Red Quills, size 14 light olive/tan/pink for Hendricksons, size 12 through 16 tannish yellow for March Brown and Gray Fox mayflies, size 14 through 20 amber, pale yellow, and tannish yellow for Sulphurs, size 10 and 12 brownish gray for Slate Drakes, size 14 and 16 light olive for the big BWO mayflies, size 8 and 10 pale yellow for Green Drakes, and size 12 through 16 cream/white for Cahills. A good idea is to plan ahead when you are traveling to a new stream and call the local fly shop—they should be able to tell you what's hatching and give you an idea as to the size and color of the local mayflies.

If you do not tie your own leaders, a 9-foot tapered leader works well for this fly. I seldom fish anything heavier than 4X or lighter than 6X for 99 percent of my dry-fly fishing. So a typical dry-fly leader for a size 14 dry fly would be the 9-foot tapered leader that ends in 4X and then a 36-inch section of 5X tippet.

- **Hook:** #10-18 ... 3035 BL...
- **Weight:** 0.015 nondescript... lead wire
- **Thread:** Black...
- **Tail:** Pheasant...
- **Rib:** Copper UTC... (brassie or small)
- **Abdomen:** Pheasant tail fibers
- **Thorax:** Peacock herl
- **Wing case:** Pheasant tail fibers
- **Legs:** Pheasant tail fibers

American Pheasant Tail Nymph

(Originator Al Troth / tier Eric Naguski)

Woolly Bugger

(Originator Russell Blessing / tier Eric Naguski)

- **Hook:** #6-12 Tiemco 5263
- **Weight:** 0.020 Lead wire
- **Thread:** Black 6/0 UNI-Thread
- **Tail:** Black marabou
- **Rib:** Copper UTC Ultra Wire (brassie)
- **Body:** Olive chenille
- **Hackle:** Black saddle hackle

The fly-fishing world became aware of the Woolly Bugger in 1984 in an article in *Fly Fisherman* magazine by Barry Beck. Created by Pennsylvania fly tier and angler Russell Blessing, the Woolly Bugger is likely one of the most productive trout flies of all time. Russell created the fly in the late 1960s, and it is often the fly that many beginning fly tiers first learn to tie. I would bet that many fly anglers' first fish on a fly rod also came on a Woolly Bugger. It may

The Woolly Bugger can be tied in as many colors as you can imagine and is as versatile as any fly that I can think of. It's an old warhorse of a fly, but, man, is it effective. A bead or cone can be added to the Woolly Bugger for some increased weight and

From the vise of Pennsylvania fly tier and angler Russell Blessing, the venerable Woolly Bugger one of the most widely used trout flies in existence.

jigging action when the fly is retrieved with short strips. Some good colors for Pennsylvania waters are all black, black and olive, all white, brown and black, all brown, rusty orange, and olive and brown. The widely available two-tone chenille, flashy chenille, and rubber legs also offer the fly tier ways to spice up their Buggers. The addition of a hot-spot collar of fluorescent orange, red, or chartreuse chenille or thread can also add to the Woolly Bugger's appeal. The possibilities are pretty much limitless.

One variation of the Woolly Bugger that is a particular standout is Cathy Beck's Super Bugger. It is hard to think of a fly that has more built-in movement and inherent "fishiness" than Cathy's Bugger. With its lead dumbbell eyes for weight and proven fish-catching jigging motion when retrieved with short strips, through the movement from the Sili Legs, hen hackle body, and marabou tail, and the Super Bugger never stops moving in the water. In all its forms, the Woolly Bugger is a fly for all times.

FISHING TECHNIQUES

In addition to the myriad ways to tie the Woolly Bugger, there are several ways to fish this fly. In its medium to small sizes, say 8 through 12, it can be fished dead-drift like a nymph. If heavily weighted it can be used to key in on emerging mayflies. Strike detection may be difficult without some kind of indicator when fishing at this shallow depth using a dead-drift presentation like you were presenting a dry fly. One method to improve your chances of seeing the take is to drop a Pheasant Tail off the back of a d pattern. This can be an extremely effec...

as an anchor fly in a multi-fly rig, or a lightly weighted (or unweighted) version can be tied to the hook of a heavy nymph like a bead-head Pat's Rubber Legs. This presentation is a productive combination, especially in the winter. Put two incredibly productive subsurface flies together, and even a sluggish winter trout may find it hard to pass up an offering like that! The Woolly Bugger can even be tied on small jig hooks and fished like a nymph.

Probably the most common and maybe the most productive method of fishing the Woolly Bugger is fishing it actively like a streamer. Vary your retrieve until you find what the fish are reacting to. One of the best times to fish a Woolly Bugger is right after a summertime rainstorm. On many hot summer days we will get an afternoon storm that doesn't last too long. I have found that the fish are incredibly responsive to a Woolly Bugger cast on the very edge of the stream (sometimes even on dry land) and then stripped quickly back. The strikes can come as soon as the fly lands or within the first foot or two of the bank, but these conditions have provided me some of the best and most exciting Woolly Bugger fishing I have ever experienced. When you do set out after a storm, cut your tippet back to 2X or 3X and be ready as soon as the fly hits the water.

This gorgeous ... an unweighted Pheasant ... nymph heavily ... emerg...

- **Hook:** #14-16 Tiemco 100BL
- **Thread:** Black 8/0 UNI-Thread
- **Tail:** Black goose biot
- **Underbody:** Black Ice Dub or black stone SLF Squirrel Dubbing
- **Overbody:** Black 0.5 mm Razor Foam
- **Underwing:** Light Dun Web Wing
- **Flash:** Opal Mirage Tinsel
- **Overwing:** Natural dun CDC
- **Legs:** Black Life Flex

Spring Creek Stone

(Originator and tier Jake Villwock)

Every March Pennsylvania's dry-fly anglers start to talk about seeing the first big aquatic flies that bring the state's trout to the surface. The early brown/black stoneflies are the year's first aquatic insects larger than a size 18 to emerge from Keystone State trout streams. It's a very spotty hatch, but in some places this insect can get the attention of enough fish to make dry-fly fishing a viable option. As an added bonus

The Spring Creek Stone is a good high-floating pattern that imitates the often-skittering adult stoneflies present in early spring in Pennsylvania.

to their larger size, the fact that they frequently emerge on the warmest sunny days in March and early April makes for a nice cure for the severe cabin fever many anglers experience over the winter.

Jake Villwock's Spring Creek Stone is a thoughtfully designed pattern for the early-season stoneflies. Typically the early stoneflies come in a dark blackish brown color, with silhouette and movement seemingly more important than exact color matching. Jake's incorporation of foam into the construction of this fly helps the angler immensely due to the fact that very often to coerce a fish into rising for your imitation, imparting some movement to the fly is crucial. This high-floating pattern of CDC and foam can be skated easily across the surface of the water. Certainly fish will eat the Spring Creek Stone on the dead drift, but frequently the movement of these stoneflies is what the trout key in to, even with the naturals. The additional movement created by the Life Flex synthetic legs only increases the effectiveness of this fly. The CDC wing provides a nice profile not unlike the fluttering wings of a stonefly moving across the surface, with just a little added flash from the Mirage Tinsel to catch a glint of sunshine to further enhance the Spring Creek Stone.

FISHING TECHNIQUES

Fished either dead drift or skated across the surface of the water on a tight line, this fly gives the early-season dry-fly angler a couple really effective presentation options. Yet another way to utilize the Spring Creek Stone's built-in buoyancy is to drop a small nymph off of the hook. This is especially effective on streams where there is a good Blue-Winged Olive population. The emergence of the early brood of BWOs often overlaps with the early stoneflies, so hanging a small BWO nymph off the Spring Creek Stone is a great way to present the BWO to the fish that are already seeing this nymph actively moving about in the water column.

On streams like Letort Spring Run, the combination of a Spring Creek Stone and a BWO nymph is a great way to have success on a stream that is notoriously difficult to fish. In the spring the fish are used to seeing the BWO nymphs up in the middle third of the water column, and since weed growth is limited this time of year, it's a great way to present nymphs in a system where nymph fishing can be challenging when the aquatic vegetation is heavy. A little dunk in High N Dry Liquid Floatant or another floatant suitable for use on CDC, and this fly is ready to go.

Signalling one of the first opportunities to fish dry flies in the spring, the early stoneflies are a welcome sight to any dry-fly angler's eyes.

Elk Hair Caddis

(Originator Al Troth / tier Eric Naguski)

- **Hook:** Tiemco 100BL sizes 10-22
- **Thread:** Camel 8/0 UNI-Thread
- **Rib:** Gold UTC Ultra Wire (small)
- **Body:** Tan Blue Ribbon Flies Zelon Dubbing
- **Wing:** Nature's Spirit Select Cow Elk Natural

Like the Woolly Bugger has caught many anglers' first trout on the fly, the Elk Hair Caddis probably accounts for many beginning fly fishers' first trout on a dry fly. Created by Pennsylvania fly tier and angler Al Troth in 1957 to match the caddisflies present on Loyalsock Creek, the Elk Hair Caddis has stood the test of time as an incredibly effective caddis and stonefly imitation and has become a staple of fly boxes across North America. With the introduction of dyed elk hair and an ever-evolving industry of genetic fly-tying hackle, it can be tied in every color and size, imitating the prevalent natural insects. It too has spawned many variations through the use of different materials, but the same basic profile is present in its progeny.

Another wonderful feature of the Elk Hair Caddis is its bouyancy and visibility due to its construction from high-floating hollow elk hair and a body of dubbing and gathered the pattern.

Another Pennsylvania classic, the Elk Hair Caddis, like the Woolly Bugger, has gained international fame in the trout-fishing world. It is a high-floating fly that bounces around on turbulent water much like a fluttering adult caddis.

Pine Creek below Slate Run, Pennsylvania. Pine Creek is big water and can have spectacular caddis hatches. A traditional Elk Hair Caddis can bring some of this creek's lovely brown trout to the surface.

hackle. The construction is such that the Elk Hair Caddis is one of the most durable dry flies around if tied properly. The durable elk hair and hackle reinforced with gold wire will stand up to several fish. I personally have had a single Elk Hair Caddis last for at least two-dozen trout in a single day. It is relatively maintenance-free as well. An initial dunk in a liquid floatant, then drying it off in amadou or a Wonder Cloth, and a little dessicant like High N Dry's powdered floatant after each fish, and the fly should last you a while, and hold on!

FISHING TECHNIQUES

This pattern performs well on a variety of water types. It will stay afloat and bounce around on a fast riffle if landed correctly and keep well on flat water, and is buoyant enough to skate and skitter the fly across the surface on a tight line if the trout seem to want a moving caddis on any particular day. The Elk Hair Caddis also makes for an effective component of the dry-dropper rig. I'm fairly certain that a Pheasant Tail or Hare's Ear Nymph dropped off the back of an Elk Hair Caddis has accounted for more than just a few trout coming to hand. Predominantly, tan and olive are the major colors to have in your box, but to cover your bases, a good size and color selection for Pennsylvania would be size 14 through 18 in tan, olive, and black, and size 10 through 16 in orange for some of the caddis present in the fall. Add the jigging action of the

A standard 9-foot tapered leader is fine to fish the Elk Hair Caddis. Early in the year you can get away with 4X tippet, but 5X and 6X may be required as the season progresses and water levels go down and clarity improves. It is not an absolute necessity, but I like to use a monofilament loop with caddis patterns. They move around a little better with an improved clinch or double Davey knot. After some practice you can get pretty good at tying a small loop.

- **Hook:** #18-24 Tiemco 2488
- **Bead:** 2 mm Silver Tungsten Bead
- **Thread:** Black Veevus 14/0
- **Rib:** Silver UTC Ultra Wire (small)
- **Body:** Black Veevus 14/0

Zebra Midge

(Originator Ted Welling / tier Eric Naguski)

The Zebra Midge is, for good reason, one of the most popular midge pupa patterns out there, and its slender profile mimics that of one of the most common food sources for trout in Pennsylvania waters. Created by Lees Ferry, Arizona, guide Ted Welling, the Zebra Midge is a midge pupa imitation that works everywhere there are midges, which is pretty much everywhere. The fly sinks quickly and is very effective used in a variety of rigs. While the black-and-silver version of the Zebra Midge is the most common, other color combinations that work well in Pennsylvania waters are gray with black wire, black with copper wire, black with red wire, and red with black wire. The bead can match the wire or the body color.

Anglers coming into the fly shop where I work frequently want advice on what flies

The diminutive Zebra Midge, Ted Welling's incredibly effective midge pupa pattern, deserves a place in every fly angler's box. Midges are ubiquitous in trout waters across Pennsylvania, and to be truly prepared, an angler should not be without this pattern.

to use. The Zebra Midge is almost always one of the flies that is recommended, especially during the heat of summer and warm days of winter when we see a lot of midge activity. In many of Pennsylvania's trout waters, midges make up a large portion of the insect biomass, so the fish are used to seeing them. In our spring creeks midge populations are very high, and the Zebra Midge is always a good starting point when there is no visible insect activity. Any angler coming to fish Pennsylvania's popular trout streams in the winter would do well to have a supply of Zebra Midges with them in a few different color combinations.

FISHING TECHNIQUES

A single Zebra Midge under a light yarn or wool indicator can be very effective when targeting suspended fish and is a good option on Pennsylvania streams like the Yellow Breeches and Tulpehocken Creek. A similar tactic is to drop the Zebra Midge off the back of a Squirmy Worm or other large attractor nymph. This can be presented as part of a tight-line nymph system or fished under an indicator. In the summer, a Zebra Midge works well dropped off the back of a terrestrial like a hopper, ant, or beetle.

The use of fluorocarbon tippet and the double Davey knot is a good tactic to limit the visibility of your connection to the fly and allows you to get away with a slightly heavier tippet than if you were using nylon tippet material.

The trout will gorge themselves on midges when they are emerging. During that time the pupae will ride in the water column at different depths, so before you change your fly pattern, a solid tactic is to vary the depth that you are fishing. This can be most easily achieved with an indicator rig. It doesn't require much wool or yarn to suspend a Zebra Midge at various depths, and moving the indicator is very simple with the right setup. The Dorsey Indicator and New Zealand Strike Indicator both do a great job of this.

The same depth control can be achieved using a tight-line system, and anglers should strive to be proficient at both tight-line nymphing and using an indicator. Domenick Swentosky has some really great thoughts on the subject of tight-line versus indicator nymphing, and I would encourage the reader to seek out his blog Troutbitten to read more.

... ...of patch ...can be ... imitated by ... ...s CDC
Trorax Dun

Recipe (Hot Spot Beadhead Hare's Ear Nymph):
- **Hook:** #10-18 Tiemco 3761
- **Thread:** Brown 8/0 UNI-Thread
- **Weight:** 0.015- or 0.020-inch-diameter lead wire
- **Bead:** Gold Tungsten Bead, sized to hook
- **Tail:** Hare's mask guard hairs
- **Rib:** Gold UTC Ultra Wire (small or brassie)
- **Abdomen:** Hare's mask fur
- **Wing case:** Turkey tail fibers
- **Thorax:** Hare's mask fur
- **Hot spot:** Fluorescent orange 12/0 Veevus

Recipe (Sticky Bun Sculpin):
- **Rear hook:** #2-8 Gamakatsu
- **Front hook:** 25 mm Flymen
- **Tail:** Barred olive Rabbit Zonker
- **Rib:** Gold Oval Copper
- **Body:** Chenille
- **Collar:** Olive mallard flank
- **Legs:** Barred olive Sili Legs
- **Collar:** 12/0 Veevus barred olive Rabbit Zonker
- **Underfin:** Sculpin olive Senyo's Laser Dub
- **Pectoral fins:** Barred olive Rabbit Zonker
- **Head:** Olive Flymen Fish-Skull Sculpin Helmet Small
- **Mohawk:** Barred olive Rabbit Zonker

Sticky Bun Sculpin
(Originator and tier Mike Williams)

Hot Spot Beadhead Hare's Ear Nymph
(Originator unknown / tier Eric Naguski)

When anglers discuss how to catch the biggest of Pennsylvania's brown trout, a sculpin pattern usually enters the conversation. And with good reason. The

I will never forget the first time I saw how effective a fly rod could be versus bait. It was opening day of trout season—I think the year was 1979 or '80—and I was fishing with a friend whose parents had a cabin in the Pocono region of Pennsylvania not too far from Promised Land State Park. As usual on the first day of trout season in Pennsylvania, trout you may encounter. Those anglers

the stream was crowded with anglers hoping to fill their limit of eight trout. I was in a spot at the lower third of a small pool on Wallenpaupack Creek. On my initial cast I hooked a fish just as my freshly tied Gold-Ribbed Hare's Ear Nymph began to swing at the end of the drift. This scenario continued for over a dozen fish. I was only eleven or twelve years is a predator. I have seen 14-inch brown

The Hare's Ear Nymph is one of the all-time-best mayfly nymph imitations, and the Hot Spot Beadhead is a stellar version of this classic fly. It matches the predominant silhouette and colors of most mayfly nymphs, and the inherent "bugginess" of the hare's mask dubbing makes this fly a time-tested winner.

The bottom-dwelling sculpin is ubiquitous in Pennsylvania trout streams. No streamer box would be complete without a good sculpin pattern like the Sticky Bun Sculpin.

old, and the noises and comments from the surrounding bait anglers every time I hooked and then released a trout were enough to make me think I knew what I was doing. Really, I had no clue, but it was just the right place, right time, right fly. The right fly was a size 14 Hare's Ear Nymph that I had learned to tie from a book.

The centuries-old use of hare's ear dubbing has withstood the test of time, and the Gold-Ribbed Hare's Ear is on most anglers' lists of top fly patterns. The Hare's Ear is typically one of the first nymphs a beginning fly tier learns to tie. Once you learn how to manipulate the materials and get the proportions correct, you have the skill set to tie many nymph patterns that have the same basic construction but incorporate different materials. Like many other productive nymph patterns, the Gold-Ribbed Hare's Ear mimics nothing specific but many things in general. The inclusion of the spiky guard hairs provides the illusion of legs, while also adding a little movement and trapping air bubbles. The inherent "bugginess" of the pattern makes it one of the top-producing nymphs of all time. Add to its historical success and basic construction the modern dyes, beads, jig hooks, hot spots, wire colors, and flash available to the modern angler and fly tier, and the variations on the theme are seemingly never-ending. If you were to combine the variations of the Gold-Ribbed Hare's Ear Nymph and the Pheasant Tail Nymph, you could fill a nymph box with a whole bunch of fish-catching patterns.

A couple favorite variations of the Hare's Ear Nymph from the people I spoke to for this book are a flashback version and a version that utilizes a tag of bright orange thread or floss for the tail. Most think of the Hare's Ear Nymph as a mayfly nymph and that certainly makes sense, but tied in larger sizes (#6-10) it becomes a serviceable stonefly nymph imitation. The Hot Spot Beadhead version shown here in sizes 14 through 18 is a go-to nymph on the Yellow Breeches and many other Pennsylvania trout streams like Penns Creek, the Little Juniata, and Broadhead Creek to name just a few.

FISHING TECHNIQUES

Like almost all of the other nymph patterns in this book, the Hot Spot Beadhead Hare's Ear Nymph can be fished as a single nymph on a tight line or under an indicator, or as part of a dry-dropper rig or other multi-fly setup. It is also a good idea to carry a few unweighted versions of this pattern. After a substantial application of a good floatant, the fly can be fished right in the film to a rising fish. This presentation has fooled more than one difficult fish. Truthfully, I don't know a single seasoned Pennsylvania fly angler that does not carry at least one version of the Gold-Ribbed Hare's Ear Nymph.

A sculpin from Fort Spring Run—a high-protein snack for any growing brown trout. The Sticky Bun gets down where these prey items live.

A traditional Gold-Ribbed Hare's Ear Nymph, one of the most effective subsurface trout patterns of all time.

- **Sulphur Version**
- **Hook:** #14-18 Daiichi 1130
- **Thread:** Light Cahill 8/0 UNI-Thread
- **Tail/shuck:** Lemon wood duck flank and brown Z-Lon
- **Abdomen:** Mottled turkey tail fibers
- **Rib:** Gold wire (small)
- **Thorax:** Orange Sulphur Jack Mickievicz Polytek Dry Fly Blend
- **Wing:** Dyed light dun CDC
- **Hackle:** Pale watery dun Whiting Dry Fly Hackle

zec

Originator ...

Ramsay's Half and Half Emerger

(Originator Henry Ramsay / tier Eric Naguski)

Henry Ramsay's 2010 book, *Matching Major Eastern Hatches*, is a classic of fly-tying rationale. About that volume Henry says, "I basically put a lifetime of my fly design thought, theory and practice out into the book. Most of the fly designs were and continue to be the result of the challenges I've encountered on the stream with selective fish and technical fishing situations." To me, as someone whose educational background is in aquatic entomology and ecology, and as a person who also has spent the

Henry Ramsay's observational skills paid off with his Half and Half Emerger. It is a well-thought-out and designed pattern that does a great job of imitating an emerging mayfly.

majority of my life trying to coax a fish onto a hook, I can relate deeply to that sentiment. Henry's fly patterns are based on intimate observation of trout food and the way the fish respond to those insects, specifically mayflies, caddisflies, and stoneflies, in all of their life stages when they are available to trout.

The Half and Half Emerger is just one of Henry's amazing mayfly patterns. Its design works for virtually all of Pennsylvania's mayflies. The contrasting colors of the turkey wing and dubbing, combined with the way the fly rides in the film with only a portion above the surface film, serve to provide an excellent imitation of a mayfly struggling to free itself from the confines of its former self. The subtle movement from the trailing shuck adds to the appeal of this pattern.

The Half and Half Emerger's design allows the observant fly angler and tier to customize the colors of the anterior portion of the pattern to match the mayflies they are hoping to encounter. A simple change of dubbing, hackle, or wing coloration can provide an entire season's worth of mayfly emergers for Pennsylvania trout streams. The Half and Half Emerger lends itself particularly well to the Ephemerellid mayflies of Pennsylvania: the Hendricksons, Sulphurs, and Large Blue-Winged Olives. In addition to those mayflies, Henry's emerger also works well for the Little Blue-Winged Olives, Blue Quills, the drakes, and late-season whiteflies and *Hexagenia* present on streams like the Yellow Breeches, Main Stem of the Delaware, and Little Juniata. The upright wing of the Half and Half Emerger makes this fly easily seen on the water and even into the low light of spring and summertime mayfly hatches. This pattern can be absolutely deadly as a Sulphur imitation when it seems like the fish will not eat anything else.

FISHING TECHNIQUES

Fishing the Half and Half Emerger is very similar to fishing any other dry fly, and a dry-fly leader with the appropriate-size tippet will work just fine. In most cases a drag-free drift is essential, and matching the size and color of the natural follows in importance when trying to fool one of Pennsylvania's picky wild fish. Allowing the fly to drift naturally into the trout's feeding lane with only the current to provide any movement to the fly is the most effective way to present it. Henry Ramsay is a custom tier and says that the Half and Half Emerger is his most frequently requested pattern. It is very easy to see why this is the case—this pattern is a wonderful rendition of an emerging mayfly dun.

Male Ephemerella subvaria, *the Red Quill—one of the mayflies well imitated by the Half and Half Emerger.*

I Can See It Midge

(Originator and tier Tom Baltz)

I think it was 1996 when I first read an article in the *Mid-Atlantic Fly Fishing Guide* about Tom Baltz's I Can See It (I.C.S.I.) Midge. At that time I was working evenings and doing a lot of midge fishing during the winter days, so the article caught my eye. Interesting how such a small thing can change fishing for someone: the I.C.S.I. Midge is one of those small things that had a huge impact on my midge fishing and thoughts on fly construction in general. I tied a few I.C.S.I. Midges up in

black and gray, and the next time out I was immediately rewarded with a few midge-eating fish from the quiet waters of the Yellow Breeches.

I often hear anglers say that they refuse to fish small flies because they are too difficult to see on the water. Well, like the name implies, this tiny fly is incredibly visible for its size and makes fishing diminutive flies less of an exercise in futility for those anglers whose eyesight may not be the greatest. Even if your eyesight is perfect,

Midge fishing made easy! The I Can See It (I.C.S.I.) Midge from Tom Baltz. Many anglers refuse to fish midges, even though they make up a large portion of a trout's diet. Tom has solved the issue of the angler having difficulty seeing the fly with the I.C.S.I. Midge.

the visibility of the I.C.S.I. Midge is a welcome trait of this fly. Well, OK, most anglers can see this fly on the water—that's already been established in its name. But if a fly doesn't catch fish, it doesn't really matter if you can see it. As Tom points out, "The first time this fly ever hit the water, a trout rose and sucked it in." Tom says that the I.C.S.I. Midge was intended to suggest a nymph or pupa just under the water's surface and is particularly useful during any emergences of small mayflies, midges, and even tiny caddisflies on both lakes and rivers. Its origin predates similar-looking European flies, and it has been the best-selling small dry fly in the Orvis catalog for many years.

Tom says that many different materials can be used for the body. Various colors of rabbit fur are excellent, and Krystal Flash makes a really neat, shiny body. Another variation for tiers who just must have tails is to double over the tag end of the tying thread as the main thread is wound rearward. After the body is wound, the doubled thread is snipped short, leaving two tails. A bit of cement on them makes them way more durable. Tom likes the two-tail version with a Krystal Flash body. The black-bodied version intended for dark midges has proven quite effective during Trico spinner falls. Try other colors too. The suggestion of a nymph/pupa stuck under the surface film holds a powerful attraction to trout. As with his Para Nymph, Tom ties the hackle in shiny side down, and the curve of the hackle takes on the shape of an upside-down umbrella.

FISHING TECHNIQUES

Tom suggests fishing this pattern on a long section of 5X or 6X tippet. The I.C.S.I. Midge can be fished dead drift like most dry flies to rising fish. I like to place the fly no more than 3 feet above my target and allow the fly to drift into the fish's feeding lane. Casting accuracy becomes paramount here, as trout that are feeding on midges will seldom move very far to feed.

Midges come in a variety of colors in Pennsylvania waters. It's always good to try to cover your bases if you can. Here is a trio of I.C.S.I. Midges in Tom's favorite color combinations.

- **Hook (abdomen):** #12-14 Daiichi 1770 swimming nymph
- **Thread:** Tan Danville's Flymaster 6/0 Nylon
- **Tails:** Natural gray ostrich herl tips
- **Rib:** Heavy cream sewing thread
- **Body:** Mix of seal brown, yellow, and cream Hareline Superfine Dry Fly Dubbing
- **Hook (thorax):** #14 Daiichi 1130 or Tiemco 2487 curved caddis
- **Body:** Mix of seal brown, yellow, and cream Hareline Superfine Dry Fly Dubbing
- **Wing case:** Turkey wing quill section
- **Legs:** Ginger mottled hen back fibers

Rothrock's Articulated Green Drake Nymph

(Originator and tier Dave Rothrock)

Here is a great mayfly nymph from veteran author, fly angler, and fly tier Dave Rothrock. Just prior to and during the famed Green Drake emergence on Pennsylvania's trout streams, one of the most consistent and productive tactics for taking some of the largest trout of the season is fishing the nymph of the Green Drake mayfly *Ephemera guttulata*. Sometime around the latter part of May, these burrowing mayflies that have been in their tunnels in the substrate of the stream for the majority of their life are now ready for a lifestyle change. As they prepare to emerge, the nymphs make a few "test runs" to the surface prior to their final ascent. The trout are keenly aware of these large insects moving about and will begin to gorge themselves on the beefy mayfly nymphs.

The large nymphs have a distinct undulating swimming action that propels them quickly through the water, and this swimming action is where Dave's articulated nymph comes in. It's easy to see why this added movement provided by the single

All the wiggle you could ask for: Dave Rothrock's Articulated Green Drake Nymph gives the nymphing angler an edge during one of the most anticipated hatches of the year in Pennsylvania.

articulation so thoughtfully incorporated into Dave's pattern makes this nymph so effective. Dave's assessment is "When tying larger patterns—the equivalent of size 10 2XL or larger—articulated nymphs have more movement and, added to the movement of gills, can suggest life." I certainly am not going to argue with that statement. When you witness the speed and undulation exhibited by a Green Drake nymph swimming to the surface, the amount of movement is plainly visible.

Dave says that when tying the Articulated Green Drake Nymph, creating the gill effect is done by plucking dubbing from the front one-half to one-third of the body, trimming out the center of the back, tinting the full length of the back with a gray marker, and allowing it to dry. After ribbing the entire body, pluck the fur bound under the rib wraps and tint with a gray marker. Attach the abdomen to the thorax hook via a piece of 5X clear monofilament, and cut the hook off at the back of the abdomen.

FISHING TECHNIQUES

There are a few options for fishing the Articulated Green Drake Nymph depending on when and where the angler is on the stream. The Green Drake nymphs like to make their homes in silty deposits behind larger rocks and boulders in the stream as well as in slow eddies and pools that collect silt. A good tactic is to locate this type of habitat in the stream and fish the fly dead drift but then allow the fly to swing across the current with a slow pulse from the rod tip.

In a shallow-enough riffle with good lighting, you will see the fish reacting to your fly. At the beginning of the drake hatch on the Little Juniata a few years ago, I was fishing a shallow riffle below the gorge on a bright, sunny afternoon and was amazed to see fish that were otherwise invisible to me suddenly leave their holding location and move several yards to chase down this pattern. It was an amazing afternoon of visual fishing that I doubt I will ever forget. When the fish begin to see the Green Drake nymphs moving about the stream, they will seldom refuse a well-placed fly.

Another location I like to concentrate on when fishing Dave's articulated nymph is in the riffle above the head of a pool. I like to cast the fly into the heaviest water at the top and tight-line the fly through the fastest water with a high-sticking method and then drop the rod tip while remaining in direct contact with the fly, allowing it to swing into the head of the pool. The strikes can come anywhere through the drift but often occur just as the fly comes out of the fastest water. The angler needs to stay in contact with the fly in this situation or strikes will go undetected.

This fly also works very well in boulder-strewn runs of somewhat slower water. Here a down-and-across presentation works well, and adding a short pulsing action with the rod tip certainly doesn't hurt. Here again, allow the fly to hang at the end of the drift, continuing to impart the pulsing action to the fly. Dave's Articulated Green Drake Nymph and its well-designed movement will be a producer wherever Green Drakes are found.

- **Hook:** #10-20 Tiemco 100BL
- **Thread:** Rusty dun 6/0 UNI-Thread
- **Shuck:** Caddis tan Z-Lon
- **Body:** Caddis tan Z-Lon dubbing
- **Wing:** Deer hair

X-Caddis

(Originator Craig and Jackie Mathews / tier Eric Naguski)

It doesn't get much simpler to tie and yet super-effective than the X-Caddis. Craig Mathews was gracious enough to spend some time speaking with me about his fly. During our conversation about the origins of the fly, he pointed out that he was trying to come up with a good pattern for emerging caddisflies. Following the success of the Sparkle Dun, Craig's wife Jackie offered the suggestion of adding the Z-Lon shuck to the fly, and thus the X-Caddis was born. Jackie also came up with the name of the X-Caddis. The silhouette created by the deer hair wing is dead-on, and the fly floats extremely well even though it rides low in the surface film. The X-Caddis is a dream come true for guides who tie their own flies. I can lose a dozen in a day, and it doesn't take me hours to replace those flies later in the evening.

Another western fly that has traveled across North America and the rest of the world, Craig Mathews's X-Caddis is a solid choice no matter where you are fishing. As long as there are caddisflies this emerger pattern is definitely worth attaching to your tippet.

It's a good idea to carry this fly in tan (#14-22), olive (#14-22), black (#14, 16, and 20), and bright green (#14-16). Those colors and sizes will cover most of the caddis you will encounter in Pennsylvania during the season. If you really want to be prepared, throw in a few orange ones in sizes 10 and 16 for those fall caddis present on many Pennsylvania streams. The Z-Lon shuck adds a little flavor to this pattern, imitating a caddis struggling to free itself from the pupal shuck.

FISHING TECHNIQUES

I like to dunk the X-Caddis in some liquid High N Dry floatant prior to fishing, and then after a false cast or two, it will ride very nicely on the water. This fly can be fished dead drift or with a little movement with the tip of the rod, causing the fly to dance a little on the surface.

Another way to present this fly is to get yourself in a position even with or slightly upstream of a rising fish, and cast the fly a short distance past the feeding lane of the fish. Pull the fly underwater prior to it getting to your target fish and then drop your rod tip, introducing a little slack in the line—the fly to pop up to the surface like an emerging caddis. Sometimes this little bit of movement can elicit a vicious strike from a hungry trout. Just try not to set the hook too soon, pulling the fly out of the fish's mouth. Often that's sometimes easier said than done.

The X-Caddis also does double duty as the dry fly in a dry-dropper rig. An X-Caddis with a caddis pupa pattern is an extremely effective combination during a caddis emergence, or even a solid option as a searching rig.

The X-Caddis can be an effective fly in the early mornings and evenings when spent caddis are on the water. Its flush-floating characteristic also allows the fly to be presented to fish that are keying in on the crippled, dead, and dying caddis. Heck, the X-Caddis also works as an emerging mayfly pattern in a color combination that matches the natural. It's hard to beat an easily tied, excellent floating, durable, and versatile dry fly like the X-Caddis.

- **Hook:** #10-16 Tiemco 450BL jig
- **Thread:** Fluorescent orange 12/0 Veevus
- **Weight:** 0.015- or 0.020-inch-diameter lead wire
- **Bead:** Silver Tungsten slotted bead
- **Rib:** Pearl Quill Body Ribbing
- **Dubbing:** Hareline Hare's Ear Plus #1

Sexy Walt's Worm

(Originator Loren Williams / tier Eric Naguski)

The Sexy Walt's, created by Pennsylvania fly fisher and tier Loren Williams, is not only a staple in most Pennsylvania fly-fishing guides' boxes but also a permanent resident in the boxes of many competitive anglers around the world. True, the Sexy Walt's is a variant of the Walt's Worm; however, due to the drastic differences in construction, the differences in the way in which the two flies are used, and the effectiveness of both flies, the Sexy Walt's Worm has, in my opinion, earned its own chapter in this book.

Another fly that is part of what is a recurring theme of this book, the Sexy Walt's is simple to tie but incredibly effective. It can be tied on a jig hook or a standard nymph hook, and there are many variations in use. I have listed a slightly different recipe than that found on Loren's website, www.lwilliamsflies.com. The recipe listed here uses a size 10 to 16 Tiemco 450BL jig hook and fluorescent orange 12/0 Veevus thread instead of the size 4 to 8 Mustad R50X and fluorescent red 6/0 Danville that Loren lists on his website. Many anglers have personal

The Sexy Walt's Worm, developed by Pennsylvania fly tier and angler Loren Williams, is so, so good and definitely more than the sum of its parts.

preferences and confidence levels in the hot-spot color, but most land on red or orange—it's hard to go wrong with either one. A crane fly larva has a subtle iridescent sheen to it, and the subtle reflective properties of the pearl rib effectively mimic this and can help in piquing the interest of the trout. Most Pennsylvania fly anglers who spend any time nymph fishing have an enormous amount of confidence in this pattern.

FISHING TECHNIQUES

From tiny blue-line brook trout streams to large tailwaters like the Delaware River, the Sexy Walt's Worm can be a productive fly for any trout water in Pennsylvania. Like the original Walt's Worm, the Sexy Walt's can be used as a single nymph or part of a multi-nymph rig under an indicator, or as part of a tight-line nymphing rig. High, dirty water may call for a Sexy Walt's on the larger end of the size spectrum fished on the soft edges, or the angler fishing contrastingly low summer flows may want to use a size 16 or 18 Sexy Walt's dropped from a dry fly as part of a dry-dropper setup. Most of the time a high level of confidence can be had with the Sexy Walt's as one of your go-to nymph patterns when picking apart a riffle on any Pennsylvania trout stream no matter what nymphing tactic you choose to use.

A fine wild brown trout from the upper reaches of Larry's Creek that could not resist a Sexy Walt's Worm.

Hackle Wing Spinner

(Originator unknown / tier Eric Naguski)

- **Rusty Spinner Version**
- **Hook:** #10-18 Hends 321
- **Thread:** Rusty dun 8/0 UNI-Thread
- **Tails:** Medium Pardo coq de leon
- **Abdomen:** Orange Polish Quills
- **Hackle:** Medium Pardo coq de leon
- **Post:** White EP Trigger Point Fibers
- **Thorax:** Mahogany Wapsi Super Fine Dubbing

The spinner fall is a highlight of a day of fishing for many dry-fly enthusiasts. It's the finale of the short-lived adult stage of the mayfly's life cycle. The dead and dying mayflies fall to the surface of the water, spent from the exertion of copulation and oviposition. These immobile mayflies become easy pickings for the trout. There are few if any other times when the angler can witness such a feeding frenzy as when a major spinner fall occurs. The stream that you were only a few minutes earlier questioning the actual presence of trout has now come alive with the riseforms of dozens of trout gorging themselves on the hapless mayflies. What a spectacle! The swarms of mating mayflies and rising trout make for what should be easy fishing. However, sometimes this scenario becomes an exercise in frustration when the trout refuse your standard poly-wing spinner patterns. This is the time for a flush-floating spinner pattern—a fly that provides the correct silhouette but is still visible to the angler. The Hackle Wing Spinner is a pattern that accomplishes both.

This pattern works for any mayfly spinner on any trout stream in Pennsylvania but really shines on those heavily pressured streams with high mayfly populations. Pennsylvania streams can get crowded and there

Forget the bushy poly-wing spinners, a Hackle Wing Spinner floats flush and floats well. Add a sighter post, and you will be ready to fool even the fussiest fish, even in the waning hours of daylight.

are few secrets anymore, so having a fly pattern that can pass muster wherever you may fish in the state is a good idea. The trout in some of our heavily pressured streams can get very picky—so picky, in fact, that they seem to reject even the naturals at times. If something doesn't seem right, they just ignore the offering, artificial or real.

The beauty of the Hackle Wing Spinner is its ability to float just in the surface film. The use of coq de leon hackle provides a stiff barbed wing that dries easily with a false cast or two. I like to pre-treat most of my dry flies with a liquid floatant like High N Dry. After a fish, a simple squeeze in a Wonder Cloth or amadou and the application of a desiccant-like fumed silica like High N Dry's powdered floatant, and you are floating again.

The body of the Hackle Wing Spinner is really up to the angler/tier. A biot or stripped quill body provides a nice, slender silhouette much like the natural mayfly spinner's abdomen. This same profile and segmentation can be achieved using a judicious amount of dry-fly dubbing and a ribbing of thread.

To match the major hatches of Pennsylvania, colors and sizes to have in your box are rusty brown size 10 through 20 for Hendricksons and Sulphurs, dark olive size 14 through 18 for Large Blue-Winged Olives, mahogany size 10 through 18 for Slate Drakes and Blue Quills, black and black and cream size 20 through 26 for Tricos, pale yellow size 12 through 20 for Cahills and Sulphurs, white size 12 through 16 for Cahills and whiteflies, and tan size 10 through 16 for March Browns and Gray Fox spinners. The pattern can be tied with or without the sighter post.

FISHING TECHNIQUES

During the main Pennsylvania mayfly emergence period, April through August on most waters, spinner falls typically occur in the evenings either just prior to or soon after sunset. There are several exceptions to this general rule, however. Mayflies like Tricos and *Drunella cornuta* (Large Blue-Winged Olives) have morning and afternoon spinner falls, even during the heat of the summer. However, for the most part, mayflies will perform their mating ritual and fall lifeless to the water soon after in the evening hours. Evening spinner falls can be frustrating fishing due to the low light and often there are several species of mayflies present at the same time. It pays to get some reliable information from local anglers or fly shops.

Fishing the Hackle Wing Spinner is pretty straightforward dry-fly fishing. A drag-free drift is paramount, and anything else will almost assuredly be ignored by the trout. In the lower light you can sometimes use a slightly heavier tippet than what you were fishing during the emergence of mayflies earlier in the day. Try to position yourself as close to the fish as possible, and present the fly only a few feet upstream of it.

Hackle Wing Spinners can also be effective early in the morning, especially directly following a heavy spinner fall the previous evening. Move slowly and look for fish rising along the banks in small eddies and soft water where dead insects collect. It can be some of the best dry-fly fishing you will ever encounter.

- **Hook:** #10-18 Tiemco 3769
- **Thread:** Chartreuse Veevus 12/0
- **Weight:** 0.015-inch-diameter lead wire
- **Body:** Chartreuse chenille (small or medium)

Green Weenie

(Originator Ken Igo and Russ Mowry / tier Eric Naguski)

I was busy with the father of a father-and-son duo that I was guiding one day on a south-central Pennsylvania stream. The father was not as experienced as his son, to whom I had handed a size 16 Green Weenie and sent upstream while I rigged up his father with the same fly and an indicator. I watched and helped as the dad missed a couple fish and then landed two out of the first pool we fished. No more than twenty minutes could have passed. I moved upstream to see how the son was doing. He met me on the path and asked me if I could give him a different fly. I said, "Sure, did you break it off in a tree?" He laughed, handed me the Green Weenie, and said, "No, but I just caught eight fish on eight casts. Can I have something that may be a little more challenging?" That's the Green Weenie . . .

Created by Ken Igo and Russ Mowry from Westmoreland County, Pennsylvania, this little chartreuse bug can be truly amazing at times. And I'm not talking about catching stocked trout. The Green Weenie, which is nothing more than chartreuse chenille wrapped around the shank of a hook, can be just as effective on the wildest of Pennsylvania's trout. I suppose some call it a "junk fly," but it has been in my fly box as long as I can remember. The Green Weenie

The Green Weenie, a funny name for a serious fish catcher. The Weenie can be an imitation of an inchworm or a caddis larva, or just a good attractor nymph.

may have a funny name, which I think it got from the green rubber hot dog Pittsburgh Pirates trainer Danny Whelan used to put a hex on opposing pitchers, but whatever you call it, it catches trout.

I can tell you from professional experience doing aquatic macroinvertebrate sampling in many streams across Pennsylvania that there are indeed bright green caddis larvae present in a lot of them, so maybe that's what the trout think the Green Weenie is. Or maybe they take it for the bright green looper caterpillar that hangs from the hemlock trees lining the banks of so many of the Keystone State's trout waters. I suppose we will never know exactly. But I can tell you without a doubt that sometimes it seems like those little green flies are like a drug to the fish.

FISHING TECHNIQUES

The Green Weenie is versatile as well. It can be tied and fished a few different ways. If you happen to be on a stream where the small looper inchworms are present, an unweighted Green Weenie treated with floatant is a good choice. You can fish this setup as you would any other terrestrial dry fly. Admittedly, it doesn't float so well, and if you are unable to sight-fish the fly in this manner, dropping it off the back of a dry fly or under an indicator may be a better tactic.

If you do fish the Green Weenie under an indicator, I would recommend a yarn-type indicator. I am a big fan of the New Zealand Strike Indicator. It lands softly, is more sensitive than a plastic indicator like a Thingamabobber, and can be easily

Bead head version of the Green Weenie. Sometimes you need to get the fly down.

moved on the leader to adjust for depth. I find the yarn-type indicator much easier to fish, especially when casting upstream, as you will typically be doing when fishing the Green Weenie on or just below the surface.

The Green Weenie also can be tied with lead wraps or with a bead. You can fish the weighted version just like you would any other nymph, with a dead-drift presentation on a tight-line system or under an indicator.

Matt Kowalchuk, who guides on Penns Creek, likes to fish the Green Weenie under a foam terrestrial like a Chubby Chernobyl. This tactic is very effective as our season in Pennsylvania progresses and we enter into summertime. That is not to say that the Green Weenie only works in the summer. It can be part of your nymph rig any time of the year and on any day be a producer.

A simple little fly that some call "junk," the Green Weenie is a Pennsylvania classic. Although it may be simple, it is indeed a fish catcher here in Pennsylvania. Fly fishing does not need to be complicated.

- **Hook:** #12-18 Tiemco 230BL
- **Thread:** Gray 8/0 UNI-Thread
- **Weight:** 0.025-inch-diameter lead wire
- **Dubbing:** Sow bug Sow-Scud Dubbing
- **Dorsal line:** Loon UV Flow

SYE Sow Bug

(Originator and tier Jake Villwock)

The SYE (Simple Yet Effective) Sow Bug comes from full-time fly-fishing guide Jake Villwock, who developed it on the spring creeks of the Cumberland Valley. It is, like its name indicates, a relatively easy fly to tie but it is a producer. When you look at the sow bugs present in our waters, they have a distinct median dark line that runs the entirety of the dorsal side of the crustacean. This dark line is faithfully reproduced in the SYE Sow Bug through the use of Loon UV Flow.

The weight of the lead wire gets the fly down where it needs to be. The color of the naturals vary from stream to stream, but a light olive gray is a good middle ground that covers your bases no matter where you are fishing. If you want to have specific patterns for certain creeks, as a general rule the sow bugs in the Cumberland Valley are

Simple yet effective—yes indeed it is. The SYE (Simple Yet Effective) Sow Bug, from the vise of Jake Villwock, is a cress bug (sow bug) pattern that every spring creek angler should carry.

more olive-colored than their gray counterparts in the central part of the state.

Sow bugs or cress bugs, whatever you want to call them, are major food items in most if not all of the limestone spring creeks in Pennsylvania. In short, if you are planning to fish Spring Creek in Centre County, or any of the spring creeks in the Cumberland Valley, make sure you have at least a few of these flies in your box. All it takes is one handful of aquatic vegetation from any of these creeks to see just how plentiful these crustaceans are in the limestone waters of Pennsylvania. The sow bugs are available to fish 365 days a year and provide a wonderful forage base for trout living in these waters. So when in doubt as to what fly to start with on these spring creeks, it's really hard to argue with using a sow bug imitation.

FISHING TECHNIQUES

I recommend fishing this fly on fluorocarbon tippet of 4X to 6X. Most of our limestone streams are exceptionally clear and the fish see a lot of flies. Jake likes to fish the SYE Sow Bug as part of a dry-dropper rig, and there is no denying this is an effective way to fish this fly. The SYE can also effectively be fished as you would any other nymph, under an indicator or as part of a tight-line technique.

If you really want to up your game, try sight-fishing a single SYE Sow Bug to a

Angler, bassist, and luthier Jack Hill shows what can happen when you have a good cress bug pattern on one of Pennsylvania's limestone spring creeks.

specific fish, and you might be rewarded by an entirely visual experience that can paint an everlasting memory. No one soon forgets the moment when a wild rainbow that looks like a steelhead feels the sting of their hook and goes berserk in the confines of a small spring creek. What was a quiet pastoral setting suddenly becomes a venue for mayhem. The SYE Sow Bug is a fly that can make those kinds of memories happen.

- **Olive Version**
- **Hook:** #14-18 Tiemco 100BL
- **Thread:** Tan 12/0 Benecchi
- **Abdomen:** Olive Wapsi Super Fine Dry Fly Dubbing
- **Underwing:** Light dun CDC
- **Overwing:** Comparadun deer hair
- **Hackle:** Grizzly tied in Hackle Stacker style

Splitsville Caddis

(Originator Jonny King / tier Eric Naguski)

Jonny King is right on the mark with this one. The Splitsville Caddis is a very versatile caddis pattern. Like the name implies, the split wing of deer hair and CDC does a great job of imitating crippled or spent adult caddisflies. The original pattern had only a deer hair wing, but the addition of the CDC underwing adds to the floatation of this fly and does so without adding too much to the silhouette. The split wing construction of the Splitsville Caddis provides a flush-floating fly, but this pattern is much more visible to the angler than a delta wing or burnt wing spent caddis while providing a very similar shape when viewed from the trout's perspective. The Hackle Stacker method of hackling the fly only adds to the floatation and visibility and provides the prominent legs of the natural. The Splitsville has become a staple not only in my guide box but in the boxes of many other anglers who fish some of the fussiest trout in Pennsylvania. The dual role that this fly can play is what really makes it a winner.

Jonny King's Splitsville Caddis hits all the right notes for a caddis pattern. Versatile and very effective, the Splitsville Caddis can emulate a struggling adult caddis trying to emerge from the water or a spent caddis after mating.

FISHING TECHNIQUES

On streams with high populations of caddisflies, especially the Spotted Sedges, the fish are used to seeing caddis at all times of the day. In the early mornings a really fun and productive tactic is to quietly walk the banks, moving upstream slowly and watching for fish rising to dead insects from the previous evening's egg-laying occurrence. These dead insects require very little effort on the fish's part, and during times of heavy hatches, there can be a significant amount of food available to the trout. The Splitsville Caddis is an excellent choice when there are bunches of dead caddisflies along the edges and back eddies of the stream. This is the lair of the bank sipper. The angler should move slowly and pay close attention to what may be only slightly perceptible rises. Some of the largest dry-fly fish of each season come from utilizing this tactic.

The Splitsville shines as well during the emergence period of the caddisflies. The pattern mimics a spent-wing cripple as well as or better than most other caddis patterns out there. Yet another tactic where the Splitsville shines is skittering it across the surface of the water, mimicking an adult crippled caddis. This typically requires a relatively short line and a down-and-across presentation. The Splitsville's deer hair and CDC wing provides enough floatation to accomplish this. At times, this presentation can really get a fish to move to your fly.

Adding the Splitsville to your caddisfly arsenal will give you a fly that can cover a few situations that occur when the caddisflies are out and about on Pennsylvania's trout waters. For matching the majority of the state's caddis hatches, I would suggest carrying the Splitsville in sizes 14 through 18 in tan, bright green, and olive and sizes 14, 16, and 20 in black.

A gorgeous Big Fishing Creek brown trout from the Narrows section of the Clinton County limestone stream. This fish was steadily eating adult caddis in the tailout of a flat pool. It ate the Splitsville Caddis on the first drift.

- **Hook:** #12-14 Daiichi 1710 2XL or Orvis Traditional Nymph
- **Thread:** Camel 8/0 UNI-Thread
- **Tails:** Brown ostrich herl tips
- **Rib:** Brown sewing thread
- **Median stripe:** White sewing thread
- **Abdomen and thorax:** Mix of seal brown, brown, and dark brown Hareline Superfine Dry Fly Dubbing
- **Wing case:** Black Poly Yarn
- **Legs:** Brown mottled hen back fibers
- **Note:** Run dubbing needle along sides of abdomen to gently pluck fur out to form gills. Trim to length and density desired.

Rothrock's Slate Drake Nymph

(Originator and tier Dave Rothrock)

Dave Rothrock spends a good bit of his time fishing the central and northern tier of Pennsylvania, and the trout waters in those areas almost all have good populations of *Isonychia* mayflies. The light-colored median dorsal stripe that is so conspicuous on most *Isonychia* nymphs is in place on Dave's pattern, and I'm convinced that the stripe serves as a trigger for the trout to recognize the fast-swimming Iso nymphs. Dave's well-thought-out nymph also incorporates the movement of the prominent lateral gills present on the Iso nymphs. Dave says that "with gills being

Rothrock's Slate Drake Nymph is a realistic nymph pattern for one of Pennsylvania's most common mayflies, the Isonychia. *Dead-drift it or swing it down and across. The fish will notice.*

such a prominent characteristic on many mayfly nymphs, I developed an entire series of fur-gilled mayfly nymph patterns back in the mid-1980s. I believe that incorporating the suggestion of gills can add to the effectiveness of these patterns. There are times when these patterns have produced trout when others have not."

It's difficult to argue with Dave's logic. When viewed up close, the gills of the *Isonychia* nymphs are constantly moving. Dave's incorporation of this anatomical feature is intuitive and spot on. This nymph has built-in movement through thoughtful design and choice of materials. The ostrich herl tails, buggy dubbing, and hen hackle fibers all provide good movement in the water.

Isonychia nymphs are incredibly strong swimmers and are frequently moving about the benthos, especially when they are emerging. It is commonly thought that all Iso nymphs crawl out on exposed rocks to shed their nymphal shucks, and for certain, many do exhibit this strategy when transforming into the subadult mayfly. But there are also some that emerge midstream. One thing I know for certain about aquatic insects: never say never or always when it comes to their behavior. Wherever they are emerging, they are swimming to get there and the trout notice.

FISHING TECHNIQUES

Probably the best tactic for fishing Rothrock's Slate Drake Nymph is a dead-drift presentation and then swinging the nymph across the current. At the end of this presentation the angler may want to allow the nymph

Isonychia *nymph underwater. Their swimming behavior and conspicuous dorsal stripe make these nymphs a recognizable food source for trout.*

to hang in the current downstream with some short movements with the rod tip perpendicular to the flow. This action serves to imitate the nymph struggling to swim against the current just below the surface. When the strikes come at this moment, they are savage!

Typically the Slate Drakes begin to emerge sometime around early June in most of Pennsylvania, but as with most things insect and fish related, they don't seem to have a calendar, and degree days and photoperiod seem to dictate when we see the adults. The *Isonychia* present in Pennsylvania have two periods of emergence, one in the summer and one in the fall. In general, the fall bugs are a little smaller than those found earlier in the year. The nymphs are present year-round, and fishing Dave's *Isonychia* nymph in streams like Pine Creek, Penns Creek, and Slate Run, along with many, many others in Pennsylvania, can be a solid choice when no mayflies are hatching. The fish are used to seeing them and recognize them as a food source.

- **Hook:** Daiichi 1100 or Daiichi 1170 sizes 14-20
- **Thread:** Black Danville's Flymaster 6/0 Nylon, waxed
- **Post:** Fluorescent orange calf body hair
- **Hackle:** Grizzly
- **Body:** Black rabbit fur dubbing

I Can See It Ant

(Originator and tier Tom Baltz)

All trout love ants. It's a fact. And there are a ton of ant patterns out there. The biggest problem with ant patterns is being able to see them on the water. Well, once again Tom Baltz has solved that problem with another fly in his I Can See It (I.C.S.I.) series of flies. His utilization of orange and yellow calf tail for parachute posts solves the visibility issue for this ant pattern. Another issue with many ant patterns is that they don't float like real ants do. Real ants typically float right in the surface film. So like the Para Nymph and the I.C.S.I. Midge, the hackle on the I.C.S.I. Ant is tied in with the shiny side facing down so really only the parachute post sticks up above the surface film. With the I.C.S.I. Ant the profile that the fish sees is as close to natural as you can get while still being very visible to the angler.

I cannot overemphasize the importance of anglers being able to see ant patterns. They are so effective but many anglers just can't see them on the water. Many of the streams in Pennsylvania are wooded and have a large amount of "dark water" caused by the shadows thrown by streamside vegetation such as hemlocks, rhododendrons, and other trees and bushes. The irony here is that this is exactly the habitat of many kinds of ants, especially the large carpenter ants commonly found in the state's forests. The I.C.S.I. Ant is perfect for these types

The hardest thing about fishing ants is seeing them on the water. Another installment in Tom Baltz's I Can See It (I.C.S.I.) series of patterns, the I.C.S.I. Ant takes the guesswork out of locating your ant pattern on the water.

of streams. Trout will hold along the banks of these streams, directly under the vegetation, as both a feeding lie and cover from overhead predators like herons and other avian threats. So during the middle and late season here in Pennsylvania, an I.C.S.I. Ant is a valuable fly to carry in your box when searching for surface-feeding trout.

FISHING TECHNIQUES

In the summertime, a fun way to escape the heat is to find a shady section of trout stream that has cold water and just blind cast an I.C.S.I. Ant to likely-looking spots while *slowly* moving upstream—did I mention that you should go slowly? Seriously, if you are throwing a bow wake while wading, your chances of spooking your quarry are very high. Look for fish holding under limbs, along logs, under overhanging branches, etc. These fish see ants in the water all the time and recognize them as an easy meal. If you do not spook them, chances are they will rise to your offering.

A long, light section of tippet is a good idea when fishing the I.C.S.I. Ant. I like 3 feet of 5X or 6X most places but will try to get away with 4X if I am using a larger ant and I think I may encounter a big fish around heavy structure.

A nicely wooded section of stream, perfect for fishing the I.C.S.I. Ant during the summer and fall.

- **Hook:** #10-18 Tiemco 3671SP-BL
- **Weight:** 0.015-inch-diameter lead wire
- **Thread:** Black 8/0 UNI-Thread
- **Tail:** Pheasant tail fibers
- **Rib:** Copper UTC Ultra Wire (brassie or small)
- **Abdomen:** Pheasant tail fibers
- **Thorax:** Peacock herl
- **Wing case:** Pheasant tail fibers
- **Legs:** Pheasant tail fibers

American Pheasant Tail Nymph

(Originator Al Troth / tier Eric Naguski)

The Pheasant Tail Nymph is likely on every angler's top ten list of flies to have, no matter where you are fly fishing for trout. Frank Sawyer's original was modified, I'd say improved, by Pennsylvania fly fisherman and tier Al Troth, the same Al Troth who invented the venerable Elk Hair Caddis. Al added a slightly beefier thorax via the incorporation of peacock herl and also added a bit of realism to the original pattern by adding the pheasant tail legs. This version may be the most used fly of all time anywhere and everywhere in the trout-fishing world. Combine its popularity with all of the derivations of the Pheasant Tail, like the Frenchie for example, and it's hard to argue that it is truly a foundation for fly tying and fly fishing around the world.

So why is the Pheasant Tail such a good fly? Well, I think all it takes is a look at the natural mayfly nymph to see why it catches fish no matter where you go. The mottled iridescence of the natural pheasant tail and its brown, black, yellow, olive, copper, and dark reddish colors are found in most mayfly nymphs. Add to that the segmentation and subtle flash provided by the copper wire, the dark contrast of the peacock herl thorax, and the legs—yes, I think the legs do make a difference. I've seen few if any mayfly nymphs that didn't have legs at least at some point in their life. I don't think we

Al Troth's American Pheasant Tail Nymph is a timeless classic that is still very much relevant today. This pattern has spawned many variations.

need super-realistic flies to catch fish, but there are certain morphological features of aquatic insects that only help when they are incorporated into a fly's design. If nothing else, the legs on the Pheasant Tail provide a small amount of movement.

With the availability of dyed pheasant tails, the creative tier can create many variations of the Pheasant Tail. The melanistic or dyed black tails are especially effective. The fibers from these tails give the tier the ability to tie the Pheasant Tail in a darker hue that is frequently found in the natural mayfly nymphs. The addition of a bead or a thread hot-spot collar is another productive variation on the original.

The Pheasant Tail really shines for Pennsylvania fishing in size 14 and smaller. A good idea is to carry this pattern in sizes 14 through 20 in weighted and unweighted versions.

FISHING TECHNIQUES

The Pheasant Tail works well as an imitation for many of Pennsylvania's mayflies and really seems to shine as an imitation for the Baetid and Ephemerellid mayflies like our Blue-Winged Olives, Sulphurs, and Hendricksons. An unweighted Pheasant Tail Nymph fished just below the surface can be just the right thing when fish are starting to key in on emerging mayflies. Strike detection may be difficult without some kind of indicator when fishing at this shallow depth using a dead-drift presentation like you were presenting a dry fly. One method to improve your chances of seeing the take is to drop a Pheasant Tail off the back of a dun pattern. This can be an extremely effective

way to take fish that are up in the water column feeding on the nymphs as they swim to the surface.

Another presentation that the Pheasant Tail Nymph seems to lend itself to is as a floating fly. Apply a liberal amount of floatant to an unweighted nymph and sight-fish it to a rising fish. Here again it may be difficult to see your fly, so watch the fish. This tactic works best at short distances, but once you have a good idea of the whereabouts of your fly and you see the fish feed, set the hook. If you are not confident enough to do this, or can't get close enough to have a good visual, using a dun imitation as an indicator is a great option. Even a small yarn or wool indicator works well in this presentation.

Of course, the Pheasant Tail Nymph works wonderfully fished as part of any other standard nymphing tactic. This fly certainly ranks up there as one of the all-time-great nymph patterns. Maybe it is the best—I'll let others debate that—but I can say for sure that it is a stalwart in most experienced fly anglers' nymph selection.

This gorgeous Penns Creek brown trout ate an unweighted Pheasant Tail Nymph heavily dressed with floatant during a Drunella cornuta *emergence.*

Flapjack Stone

(Originator and tier Jake Villwock)

- **Hook:** #4-6 Partridge K12ST Sedge Caddis
- **Thread:** Camel 6/0 UNI-Thread
- **Weight:** 0.035-inch-diameter lead wire
- **Tail:** Brown Life Flex
- **Rib:** Copper brown UTC Ultra Wire (brassie)
- **Underbody:** Golden Stone Buggy Nymph Yarn
- **Shellback:** Tan 0.5 mm Razor Foam with tan mottled oak Wapsi Thin Skin
- **Legs:** Lemon barred wood duck
- **Wing case/head:** Tan 0.5 mm Razor Foam with tan mottled oak Wapsi Thin Skin
- **Antennae:** Brown Life Flex

Here is another fly from Relentless Fly Fishing owner Jake Villwock. Jake has become one of Pennsylvania's most innovative fly tiers, and although he may be known primarily as a smallmouth bass guide, he is just an all-around fishy guy, and one hell of a fly tier. Jake has been guiding for trout here in Pennsylvania for as long as he's been guiding for smallmouth bass, and he is obsessed with stoneflies.

The Flapjack Stone is an interesting and effective combination of natural and synthetic materials. What's really interesting about the construction is Jake's method of laminating Thin Skin to Razor Foam to construct the wing pads and dorsal thoracic segments of the stonefly nymph.

The Flapjack Stone is a semi-realistic pattern intended to imitate the Golden Stoneflies (Perlidae) and Yellow Stoneflies

Jake Villwock's Flapjack Stone is another wonderful stonefly nymph pattern from a Pennsylvania guide, fly tier, and angler. The Flapjack Stone is a great imitation of the Perlidae and Perlodidae stoneflies present in many of Pennsylvania's trout streams.

(Perlodidae) so prevalent in many of Pennsylvania's trout streams. The Golden Stones are found wherever there is clean water and medium to large cobble and larger substrate. Streams like Penns Creek, Pine Creek, Big Fishing Creek, and the Little Juniata all have good populations of these stoneflies. While the adult stoneflies may not have the impact on dry-fly fishing that they do in the western part of the United States, the nymphs are present in large numbers in the waters of the East and the trout recognize them as a consistent food source. Fly anglers in the Keystone State would be missing out if they choose to ignore them as an option when nymph fishing the trout streams of Pennsylvania, especially those in the central and northern portions of the state where stonefly populations are the highest.

FISHING TECHNIQUES

Jake likes to fish the Flapjack Stone anywhere there are stoneflies and typically uses a tight-line presentation with the Flapjack as the second fly in a two-fly rig, above an anchor fly. Although the Flapjack is a weighted fly, it doesn't sink as quickly as some other stonefly nymphs. This feature is especially useful during periods of high water. I like a big fly during these conditions, something the fish can see. When the water is ripping, many times the fish will move to the edges and slower current seams, so I will fish these areas when I think conditions dictate. The Flapjack Stone is a good choice

A stonefly nymph from Penns Creek. The Flapjack Stone is an excellent imitation of many different stoneflies.

for these areas of slightly slower water—the fly will stay off the bottom most of the time, but yet is visible and recognizable to the fish. The Flapjack Stone is a pattern to keep in mind when the flows are up, the water is off-color, and many other anglers have chosen to stay at home.

Another presentation for fishing the Flapjack Stone is under an indicator in slow, deep pools. This tactic is well suited for larger streams and rivers where wading is difficult or just plain impossible, and it has proved itself to me while wading portions of rivers like the Main Stem of the Delaware and Penns Creek's deepest pools. The midsection of a pool with large underwater boulders just downstream from the faster head of the pool is a prime location for this tactic, and the fish find it difficult to resist a hearty meal like a Golden Stonefly nymph drifting along in the current.

Lite Brite Zonker

(Originator Bill Black / tier Todd Johnson)

- **Hook:** #6 Daiichi 2220
- **Thread:** Black 6/0 UNI-Thread
- **Bead:** Gold tungsten (³⁄₁₆-inch)
- **Dubbing:** Black rabbit, baitfish black, and bronze Lite Brite Dubbing
- **Wing:** Black rabbit strip
- **Collar:** Red Lite Brite Dubbing
- **Head:** Black rabbit, baitfish black, and bronze Lite Brite Dubbing in front of bead

A variant of the original Zonker, the Lite Brite Zonker was originated by Bill Black of Spirit River tying materials. Feathered Hook Guide Service head guide Matt Kowalchuk's enthusiasm for this fly was contagious when I first spoke to him about his favorite streamer patterns. Matt was singing the praises of the Lite Brite Zonker that Todd Johnson ties. Apparently, I must live under a rock, because before talking to Matt and researching flies for this book, I had never heard of the pattern. But when I started digging into it, I didn't have to go too far to read and hear rave reviews about its ability to catch fish.

Todd Johnson not only was gracious enough to supply the fly for this book but also kind enough to speak to me about the Lite Brite Zonker. He spoke of how the guides at the Feathered Hook incessantly badgered him to tie the fly due to the success they were having on Penns Creek with the pattern. Todd is a Pennsylvania commercial tier who has had his flies featured

The Lite Brite Zonker is an under-the-radar streamer pattern that might just change your world.

in George Daniel's book *Strip-Set* and supplies many of the dry flies and streamers found in the bins at the Feathered Hook in Coburn, Pennsylvania. Since I personally don't buy many commercially tied flies, I never really looked closely at the flies in the shop, but when I was doing research for this book and picking up a few of Todd's Lite Brite Zonkers, I took a closer look at his work. Todd is without a doubt an extremely talented tier and should be commended on his consistency and beautifully constructed flies.

Since talking to Matt and Todd, I have added the Lite Brite Zonker to my fly box, and it has lived up to Matt's ringing endorsement. In smaller sizes (#8-10) the fly has been extremely effective for me on the streams of the Cumberland Valley during periods of high, off-color water. Effective not only in my home waters of the Cumberland Valley, the Lite Brite Zonker tied in black and red also has been a solid choice when fishing streams like Penns Creek, the Little Juniata River, and Spring Creek in Centre County when they are running a little high and off-color, especially right after and even during a heavy rain. Cast tight to the bank, or around some in-stream structure, and hold on!

The original Zonker was created by Colorado-based fly shop owner, fly tier, and angler Dan Byford in 1975. The Zonker not only gained popularity for trout in North America, but its effectiveness enamored anglers around the globe. The profile and inherent movement of the rabbit strip used as the "wing" for the Zonker is really what makes it a classic pattern that still holds its own. The Lite Brite Zonker builds on the foundation of the original Zonker, enhancing the pedigree and making the Zonker wing as relevant and effective today as it was in the 1970s and '80s.

FISHING TECHNIQUES

A standard streamer leader tapered down to 1X or 2X with a tippet of 2X or 3X will work perfectly for presenting this fly. Not only is the Lite Bright Zonker effectively fished stripped as a streamer, but it also works very well fished dead drift. Depending upon the color of the fly, the fish may take it for an injured or dead baitfish, a hellgrammite, or a crayfish. It can be tied in many color combinations. Matt Kowalchuk likes the black and red but says he will switch to the olive if the fish are not on the black. On Pennsylvania waters like the West Branch of the Delaware when flows are high and there is water spilling over the dam, alewives are washing over too. Most of these small baitfish are dead or dying, and a simple dead-drift presentation with an all-white or gray-and-white Lite Brite Zonker can be very effective.

The movement of the rabbit strip is a proven winner. Add the jigging action of the bead up front and the flash of the dubbing, and it all adds up to a fly that will get down into the strike zone and grab the fish's attention. A dead-drift presentation can be especially effective in the spring creeks of the Cumberland Valley and during the winter in the deepest runs of creeks such as Penns Creek and Big Fishing Creek. Matt says that the Lite Bright Zonker was his "first favorite streamer." Sounds like a ringing endorsement to me!

- **Hendrickson Version**
- **Hook:** #14 Tiemco 100BL
- **Thread:** Olive dun 8/0
  UNI-Thread
- **Tails:** Dark gray Microfibetts
- **Abdomen:** Hendrickson
  Nature's Spirit Turkey Biot
- **Thorax:** Light Hendrickson
  Jack Mickievicz Micro-Fine
  Blend Dry Fly Dubbing
- **Wing:** Natural dark dun CDC
- **Hackle:** Medium brown dun
  Herbert Miner

Ramsay's CDC Thorax Dun

(Originator Henry Ramsay / tier Eric Naguski)

With an honest and sincere nod to the father of modern dry-fly fishing, Henry Ramsay humbly attributes the design of his incredibly effective CDC Thorax Dun to Vince Marinaro. Vince's classic Thorax Dun was developed after hundreds of hours observing the mayflies and wild brown trout of the famed Letort Spring Run in Carlisle, Pennsylvania. Henry's CDC Thorax Dun is a wonderful adaptation of Vince's fly. It's a modern dry fly with its DNA in the past. The thoughtfulness of its construction is typical of Henry's flies and is perfect for the calm, flat pools of Pennsylvania's most technical and difficult trout streams.

Henry has taken crucial elements of Vince's Thorax Dun—the prominent wing, the slender body, and the V-shaped cutout on the underside of the hackle—to produce a dry fly that lands quietly on the water,

Presenting an almost perfect mayfly silhouette, Henry Ramsay's CDC Thorax Dun updates Vince Marinaro's Thorax Dun and provides the hatch-matching angler a highly customizable pattern to match any of Pennsylvania's mayflies.

floats well, and has the correct profile just like Vince's does. I would say that through considerate thought, Henry has updated and improved the thorax-style dry fly. Through his use of CDC, turkey biot, and modern hackle and dubbing material, he has produced an easier to tie and better floating yet equally effective dry fly.

The bug geek in me loves the use of the biot for the abdomen of the fly; the natural segmentation the material provides when wound around the hook shank is a wonderful re-creation of the segmentation found on the abdomen of the real insect. I realize that there are plenty of dry flies out there that do not have this segmentation and still catch fish, but if one can easily create this feature of the natural insect by the thoughtful use of a natural fly-tying material, why not do it? It can only serve to make a better imitation of the real thing.

On many Pennsylvania waters, the fish see *a lot* of flies. Anything a person can do, no matter how small, to improve a fly's construction or its profile is usually worth doing. Certainly there are superfluous things that can be lashed to a hook, but Henry has none of them here. The beauty of Ramsay's CDC Thorax Dun is that everything it has it needs, and there is nothing that it doesn't need. The profile of the Thorax Dun is probably its strongest feature. The silhouette of the upright wing is crucial when the trout are feeding on duns. The use of CDC is intelligent, because it has the width needed to imitate the natural mayfly wing, it is light, and with a little care, it floats extremely well. The split tails help the fly have the correct "attitude" and

float well, lying in the surface film, with the hackle trimmed on the ventral portion of the fly.

FISHING TECHNIQUES

Fishing the CDC Thorax Dun is like fishing any other dry fly. Keep drag at a minimum, or better yet, nonexistent, and this fly will be a winner for you. Just because the CDC Thorax Dun was designed for picky fish on super-flat water doesn't mean it is not an option elsewhere. This pattern floats well and really could be a go-to confidence dry fly no matter where you find fish rising to mayflies.

Henry offers the CDC Thorax Dun in Baetis Olive size 18 and 20, Early Blue Quill size 16 and 18, Light Cahill size 14, Quill Gordon size 12 and 14, March Brown size 12XL and 14XL, Cornuta Olive size 12 and 14, Hendrickson size 12 and 14, Pale Sulphur size 14 through 18, Isonychia size 12XL and 14 XL, Red Quill size 14, and Sulphur size 14 through 18.

Sulphur dun, Ephemerella invaria—*one of Pennsylvania's best hatches. This mayfly can be perfectly imitated by Ramsay's CDC Thorax Dun.*

Sticky Bun Sculpin

(Originator and tier Jake Villwock)

■ **Rear hook:** #2-8 Gamakatsu B10S
■ **Front shank:** 25 mm Flymen Articulated Shank
■ **Tail/body:** Barred olive Rabbit Zonker
■ **Underbody:** Olive copper UV Polar Chenille
■ **Collar:** Olive mallard flank
■ **Legs:** Barred olive Sili Legs
■ **Collar:** Mallard flank over barred olive Rabbit Zonker
■ **Underfin:** Sculpin olive Senyo's Laser Dub
■ **Pectoral fins:** Barred olive Rabbit Zonker
■ **Head:** Olive Flymen Fish-Skull Sculpin Helmet Small
■ **Mohawk:** Barred olive Rabbit Zonker

When anglers discuss how to catch the biggest of Pennsylvania's brown trout, a sculpin pattern usually enters the conversation. And with good reason. The mottled sculpin (*Cottus bairdii*) is found in most trout streams in Pennsylvania, and they are usually present in high numbers.

There are two big trends in trout fishing today: streamer fishing and tight-line nymphing. Tight-line nymphing because of the numbers of fish you can catch, and streamer fishing because of the truly giant trout you may encounter. Those anglers who chase big trout generally are those who "throw meat." It makes sense. As brown trout grow larger, their diet switches from one that is primarily composed of insects to one that is primarily made up of fish. A large brown trout is a predator, no doubt about it. Heck, even a small brown trout is a predator. I have seen 14-inch brown

The bottom-dwelling sculpin is ubiquitous in Pennsylvania trout streams. No streamer box would be complete without a good sculpin pattern like the Sticky Bun Sculpin.

trout puke up 6-inch brown trout that they have eaten. So if your intent as an angler is to consistently catch the biggest brown trout around, it is hard to argue against presenting them with what they want—another smaller fish. Since sculpins are so prevalent in Pennsylvania's trout waters, it makes perfect sense to have a good sculpin pattern in your arsenal of streamers.

Jake Villwock's Sticky Bun Sculpin is an articulated sculpin pattern that has everything you would want in a sculpin pattern: weight to get it down (sculpins are bottom-dwelling fish), prominent pectoral fins, a mottled brown-olive color, a flattened head thanks to the lead Sculpin Helmet, and a little flash for "look at me" flair. Like all of Jake's patterns, everything on the hook of the Sticky Bun is there for a reason. It all comes together to make a sculpin pattern with an absolute ton of movement, even when sitting still on the bottom, thanks to the use of the rabbit strip and Sili Legs, and the pectoral fins are propped out by his incorporation of Laser Dub as an under-fin. Everything about the Sticky Bun says trout food.

FISHING TECHNIQUES

I like to fish Sticky Bun Sculpins as small as a size 8 up to a size 2. A stout leader is in order. Jake recommends a 6-foot leader tapered down to 0X, a swivel, and then a tippet of 1X or 2X for a size 2 Sticky Bun. When using a smaller fly, you can go just slightly lighter with the tippet. For a size

6, a 7½-foot 1X tapered leader and 2X or 3X tippet works well. This is a heavy fly, and the size 2 casts best with a 7-weight or even 8-weight rod. Again, if you choose a smaller fly, you may be able to use a 5- or 6-weight rod.

Sculpins like to live in and around structure like rocks, boulders, submerged logs, and weed beds. Concentrating your fishing on these and other likely-looking areas is a good idea. A short strip, strip, pause retrieve effectively imitates the natural swimming action of a sculpin. They dart from one spot to the next, stopping with their pectoral fins out to the side.

For big waters the Sticky Bun may be best fished with a sinking or sink-tip line. On smaller streams a floating line works fine. Work the undercut banks of our spring creeks with a Sticky Bun, and you may just find yourself attached to a brown trout of massive proportions.

A sculpin from Letort Spring Run—a high-protein snack for any growing brown trout. The Sticky Bun gets down where these prey items live.

- **Hook:** #14 Tiemco C300BL
- **Thread:** Black 8/0 UNI-Thread
- **Rib:** UTC Ultra Wire size Brassie
- **Weight:** 0.020-inch-diameter lead wire
- **Bead:** 2.8mm Black Tungsten Bead
- **Overbody:** Olive brown Z-Lon
- **Abdomen:** Olive TroutHunter CEN Dubbing
- **Thorax:** Dark brown SLF Spikey Squirrel

Czech Nymph

(Originator unknown / tier Eric Naguski)

Most of Pennsylvania's trout streams are loaded with net-building and free-living caddis of the families Hydropsychidae (Spotted Sedge) and Rhyacophilidae (Green Sedge), respectively. And few flies simulate the larvae of these caddisflies better than a Czech Nymph. Rather than a specific pattern, the Czech Nymph is a style of nymph. Typically it is heavily weighted and is fairly simple to tie. Often a Czech Nymph will serve as an anchor fly in a two- or three-fly nymphing rig, but it can certainly be fished

solo. The ease with which this pattern is tied is a benefit, because typically an angler will be fishing this fly close to the bottom and it will hang up. You will lose some flies. A simple-to-tie pattern makes losing flies a little less painful.

The most frequently encountered colors of the free-living and net-building caddis larvae are olive and green, so it makes sense to carry at least those two colors in your box. The larvae of these two caddisfly families are available to trout almost year-round,

Caddis larvae are always present among the benthos of a trout stream. The Czech Nymph gets down and stays there where the larvae live.

so the utilization of this pattern as a searching pattern is a good idea. On many Pennsylvania streams the numbers of Spotted Sedges are massive—often they make up a majority of the insect biomass due to the fact that many of the species are somewhat tolerant of pollution. Streams like Tulpehocken Creek and the Lackawanna River come immediately to mind as Pennsylvania trout waters with huge populations of these caddisflies. That is not to say that these are the only types of streams that have these caddis. It is quite the opposite—the Spotted Sedges are ubiquitous throughout the Keystone State's waters. On streams like Penns Creek it is always a good idea for the nymph angler to consider a green or olive Czech Nymph as an option.

The name Czech Nymph comes from the realm of international competitive angling. The Czech nymphing technique—which is really just a short, tight line technique—was actually first utilized by Polish anglers in 1984. At the time, one of the other teams in the competition was the Czech team, which picked up on the technique and the flies the Polish anglers were using. The phenomenon took off after the Czech anglers used the short-line technique with these caddisfly

A bright green Rhyacophila *sp. caddisfly larva. These caddis larvae do not build a case and are free-roaming along the stream bottom. This makes them easily dislodged and thus readily available to trout.*

imitations to gain considerable success in international competition.

The original Czech Nymphs used peacock herl for the dark backs of the flies. Today there are hundreds of Czech Nymph patterns utilizing all kinds of modern materials, but a simple heavily weighted olive or green caddis larva imitation serves as a great fly for most of Pennsylvania's trout waters. The Czech Nymph fishes extremely well as part of a tight-line system but can be fished successfully under an indicator as well.

Martinez Black Jig Variant

(Originator unknown / tier Eric Naguski)

- **Hook:** #14-16 Tiemco 450BL
- **Bead:** 2.5-2.8 mm Copper slotted tungsten
- **Weight:** Seven or eight turns of 0.015-inch-diameter lead wire
- **Thread:** Black 8/0 UNI-Thread
- **Tails:** Guinea fowl
- **Rib:** Copper UTC Ultra Wire (small)
- **Abdomen:** Black beaver dubbing
- **Thorax:** Insect green Ice Dub
- **Hackle:** Partridge
- **Collar:** Black beaver dubbing

A classic nymph, the Martinez Black has been a staple in many fly boxes for decades. The original was designed in the 1940s by Don Martinez, an angler and fly tier in West Yellowstone, Montana. He was also the originator of the Woolly Worm and is considered a forefather of dry-fly fishing in the West. The original Martinez Black remains a productive fly to this day, and many experienced anglers and guides still rate it as one of the top nymphs ever.

The version here, the Martinez Black Jig Variant (MBJV), is an updated variation that has been very productive in all parts of Pennsylvania. I'm not sure if the fish are taking this fly as a cased caddis or just a dark mayfly nymph that looks like food, but I suppose it doesn't matter as long as they eat it. The dark body and contrasting bright green collar serve as a wonderful fish attractor. The fish are used to seeing both dark

The jig variant is a modern take on the classic nymph pattern the Martinez Black.

mayfly nymphs and bright green caddis larvae in most of the streams of Pennsylvania, and this may explain the performance of this fly all around the state.

I am not the only firm believer in the jig hook and its ability to hook fish but also hang up on the bottom less frequently than a standard down-eye hook. I typically tie and fish this fly in sizes 14 and 16. I also tie and fish it with a black bead in addition to the copper bead shown.

The original Martinez Black, a classic western nymph that works everywhere.

FISHING TECHNIQUES

Like many other jig nymphs, the MBJV can be fished as part of a tight-line rig, under an indicator, or as the dropper in a dry-dropper rig. If it is fished as part of an indicator rig, I prefer the sensitivity and unobtrusive landing of a wool indicator like the New Zealand Strike Indicator. This indicator rig seems to spook the fish less than the plastic indicators. The effectiveness of this fly can be fully realized using a tight-line presentation. This method really allows the angler to pick apart any likely-looking trout water. When fishing this and other nymphs on a tight-line rig, the abrasion resistance and decreased visibility of fluorocarbon tippet material are worth the extra expense.

This pattern sinks relatively quickly and is great for fishing places like the Little Juniata Gorge and the riffle sections of Penns Creek, Pohopoco Creek, Pine Creek, and Broadhead Creek, to name just a few. It is also a good choice as a dropper under a terrestrial pattern during the summer.

INDEX

ABOUT THE AUTHOR

Eric A. Naguski has spent the last forty years chasing trout around Pennsylvania with a fly rod in hand. He is the owner/guide of Riseforms Fly Fishing and a guide for Relentless Fly Fishing and Tulpehocken Creek Outfitters in Boiling Springs, Pennsylvania. Eric has a BS in Biology from Millersville University, where he concentrated on aquatic ecology and entomology. He is also the manager of the Dauphin County Conservation District and serves on the board of directors of the Cumberland Valley Chapter of Trout Unlimited and the board of the Pennsylvania Fly Fishing Museum Association. Eric resides in Boiling Springs with his wife, Margaret. They have two children, Isabelle and Henry.